HOW TO TEACH BEHAVIOUR AND HOW NOT TO

Dean Cotton

Edited by John Urwin

Positive Behaviour Strategies Ltd

Copyright © 2017 Dean Cotton

All rights reserved. This book or any portion thereof
may not be reproduced or used in any manner whatsoever
without the express written permission of the publisher
except for the use of brief quotations in a book review.

First Published 2017

ISBN 978-1542362290

Positive Behaviour Strategies Ltd
5 Cavendish Road
Sheffield
S11 9BH

www.pbstraining.co.uk

Table of Contents

Introduction 4

Almost a Century of Behavioural Problems 9

Controlling Behaviour 16

Focusing on Behaviour 40

Teaching Behaviour 47

Arousal Spectrum 60

Post Incident Learning and Support (PILS) 85

Post Incident Learning and Support (PILS) for individuals with communication difficulties 118

Appendices 150

References 153

INTRODUCTION

Positive behaviour is highly subjective and idealised. We spend an incredible amount of time comparing children to an idealised version of themselves and of course children sometimes cannot achieve the goals we set, this itself can be challenging for adults and leave them feeling negative and frustrated. This book explores the common behaviours that challenge children and practitioners and helps people look at such behaviours differently to provide a more calculated consistent approach to teaching individuals self-control.

People often say that their school years were the best years of their lives, this was not the case for me. In fact, I can quite honestly say that my school days were among the worst days of my life. In today's education system, I would have almost certainly been labelled as having Attention Deficit Hyperactivity Disorder (ADHD), but this was the 1970s and ADHD had not been invented.

Upon leaving school, I was told that 'I was a nice lad but I would never get anywhere', who was I to argue? When I left school in 1987 I thought I would never step foot in another school again.

After leaving school I had many jobs, none of which I regret, from building reproduction antique furniture, to filling gas bottles, to my first business, DWCS - Dean's Window Cleaning Services 'We rub a little harder'. At the age of 19 I became a driver for a parcel company, delivering parcels around the United Kingdom, covering around three to four hundred miles a day. This job gave me lots of time to think about my future and what I wanted to do with it.

One Thursday afternoon, I found myself delivering a parcel to a school in Sheffield. It was evident upon entering the school that this school was different, this was a special school; it was special because the staff in the school were special; this was evident from the moment I stepped foot into the school. I had never experienced a friendly, welcoming and relaxed atmosphere. The head of the school signed for the parcel I was delivering and I felt so comfortable that I asked him how I could get a job there? He told me that I could arrange to come and do some voluntary work in the school.

The very next day I turned up at the school at 9am on that Friday morning. This turned out to be one of the best decisions I have ever made. In those days, the Disclosure and Barring Service

(DBS), or the Criminal Records Bureau (CRB) did not exist. The head asked me where I would like to work in the school and, because my mother was a child-minder at the time, looking after young children, I decided that I would like to work in the school's nursery. The head showed me to the nursery and introduced me to the staff. I had a great time with the children building towers out of wooden blocks, painting pictures with our fingers and reading stories to groups of children. At lunchtime, I found myself sat in the staffroom surrounded by teachers eating their lunch from Tupperware boxes and talking about their previous evening, the head entered the room and asked me if he could 'have a word?' I followed him to his office, feeling quite concerned, I had been in many head teacher's offices before, but usually because I had done something wrong. The head teacher told me that the nursery staff had felt that I had a natural empathy with the children in the nursery and he wondered if I wanted to do some training to become a nursery nurse? I thought this was a great idea, so he immediately contacted Sheffield college who ran the National Nursery Examination Board (NNEB) training course. That same afternoon I went for an interview at Sheffield college and started the NNEB course on the following Monday. The course was full time for two years, so I took to the stage to support myself, my parents were also very supportive as always.

During my time at Sheffield college I was fortunate to work in a huge variety of service settings including the Sheffield Children's Hospital. It was here I first became interested in behaviour. I found it very interesting to see how young people can often regress when they are in hospital and I was keen to find the best ways to support them. I also experienced some prejudice being a male in what is predominantly a female role, I was the only male in three groups of around 30 women.

For the next eight years I worked in a mainstream primary school as a Nursery Nurse and my interest in behaviour developed further into a curiosity with a need to explore better ways of supporting young people. In 1999 I applied for the position of behaviour management co-ordinator at a school for young people with emotional and behavioural difficulties (EBD). It was here where I would 'learn my craft'. It is said that we learn more from mistakes than we do our successes and I made some mistakes whilst working with these young people, luckily with no disastrous results. I was also very lucky to work in a school with such fantastic colleagues who were very keen to make the school the best it could possibly be. The head of the school was an inspiration and was dedicated to the professional development of the staff team. I attended many training courses whilst working at the EBD School including a Team Teach tutor course. Team Teach is a holistic approach to behaviour management; with a primary focus on diversion, de-fusion and de-escalation, the approach also includes safe humane physical interventions. There are many training packages in this area but Team Teach was the chosen approach in our school. Following the Team Teach training and a range of other training the school received, the school went from strength to strength and behaviour in the school improved dramatically; serious incidents in the school were reduced by 95% and exclusions reduced to zero. The reduction in incidents and exclusions earned the school many accolades and in 2005, as part of a reorganization of EBD provision in the city, the school closed and two new SEBD (social, emotional, behavioural difficulties) schools opened. Following numerous calls from other services requesting training in behaviour management I decided to leave my job and start my own company 'Positive Behaviour Strategies Ltd'. In 2011 I started studying behaviour at Leicester University. I completed a Masters Degree in 2014 and I have been an independent researcher ever since.

"Choose a job you love, and you will never have to work a day in your life."
Confucius (551–479 BC)

Almost a Century of Behavioural Problems

To understand where we are today in relation to behaviour management, it is important to know where we have come from and how we got here. The last one hundred years have seen a huge array of initiatives in behaviour management, some have been very successful, some less so.

The 1921 Education Act allowed Local Education Authorities (LEAs) to pay for provision at independent schools. Some independent schools for the 'maladjusted' opened. A wave of new thinking arose from the likes of Montessori, whose methods are characterised by emphasising self-directed activity; Froebel, who introduced play as a means of engaging young people in self-activity; Steiner, who aimed to provide an unhurried and creative learning environment. In addition, the 1921 Act saw the introduction of therapeutic communities; these viewed the role of the adult as a good parent, setting boundaries and encouraging the child to face consequences. Therapeutic communities can be very effective for people with relationship and /or social difficulties as the community encourages the service users to take responsibility for their own situation and work alongside others, thus forging relationships. The philosophy of therapeutic communities is that the client takes responsibility for their own problem and is a participant in other service user's rehabilitation. Therapeutic communities gain a reputation of service user satisfaction and success in the United Kingdom and abroad.

The Education Act 1944 required full provision for pupils with special educational needs. One result was the introduction of off-site tutorial classes. The classes were informal and the teachers were allowed time to work with parents. The Act also identified 'maladjustment' as one of eleven categories of handicap. In 1947 children with behavioural problems, labelled 'maladjusted', were cared for in 5 special schools. By 1964, 2440 children attended 60 such schools (Cole and Pritchard, 2009). In 1955 the Underwood Report of the Committee on Maladjusted Children made 97 recommendations aimed at improving services for the maladjusted, the report emphasized the role of psychology services and focused on preventing problems from arising by supporting families.

The 1981 Education Act radically changes people's conceptions of special educational need (SEN). Prior to the 1981 Educational Act sending a child to a maladjusted school had to be signed off by a doctor, but the 1981 Education Act moved the model from a medical one than educational one. The Act also abolished the terms 'maladjustment' and 'handicapped' and introduced the term Emotional and Behavioural Difficulties (EBD) and Special Educational Needs (SEN) (DfE, 1994). The changes introduced new ways of thinking and created an ethos of care and inclusion.

The 1989 Elton Report (DES, 1989), reviewed behaviour in schools following a spate of stories in the press that suggested schools were in crisis, pupils were violent and much of the violence was aimed at teachers. The report found there was a persistent problem of low-level disruption and only a small minority of pupils have severe behaviour problems and the needs of such pupils cannot be met in mainstream schools.

In 1989 the children's act was published closely followed by the UN Convention on the Rights of the Child in 1991. The media's interpretation of this legislation, focused on young people's rights with little focus on their responsibilities. For the first time, we started hearing young people say something that we had not heard before "You cannot touch me, I know my rights". Although young people have rights, they also have responsibilities and one of these responsibilities is to keep themselves safe. On the other hand, staff in schools have a duty of care. When young people are not keeping themselves safe, staff might need to touch individuals to keep them safe. Guidance released in July 2013 stated that it is not illegal to touch pupils and outlined examples of where touching a pupil might be necessary:

- Holding the hand of the child when going to assembly or when walking together around the school
- When comforting a distressed pupil
- When a pupil is being congratulated or praised
- To demonstrate how to use a musical instrument
- To demonstrate exercises or techniques during PE lessons or sports coaching and to give first aid.

Department for Education July 2013

The 1993 Education Act Introduced Pupil Referral Units (PRUs) as short-term alternatives for young people who were out of school or not gaining qualifications. Although PRUs were introduced as a revolving door service, where young people would be given intensive support and then re-introduced into mainstream, this can prove difficult to achieve, as some schools are reluctant to reintegrate young people and the revolving door stops. The popularity of such services increased tenfold over the next 15 years. In 1995, 5043 children attended Pupil Referral

Units (PRUs). Section 550b of the Education Act (1996) seemed to change the way behaviour was managed and started focusing on punishments for behaviour and stated that any pupil under the age of 18 attending a school maintained by a local education authority, a city technology college, city college for the technology of the arts or an academy, can be placed in detention without the parents' consent. In 1998, 7740 children attended PRU's and over 11500 children attended day and boarding special schools. By 2007 the number of pupils labelled as SEBD had grown to 139,310 and one year later this figure had reached 149,049 (Cole and Pritchard, 2009).

In 2012 the Department for Education brought out the Behaviour and Discipline in school's guidance, A guide for head teachers and school staff. This guidance provided advice to head teachers and school staff on developing the school behaviour policy, it explained the powers members of staff have to discipline pupils. The guidance explained that it is for individually maintained schools to develop their own behaviour policies, but offers little in the way of advice into the content of a good behaviour policy. This guidance replaced earlier related DCSF guidance 'School discipline and pupil behaviour policies – guidance for schools 2010'. In 2014 the Special Educational Needs and Disability Code of Practice, recognized that young people experiencing a wide range of social and emotional difficulties, might also have underlying mental health difficulties. The Act stated that schools should have a clear process in place to support such pupils.

A brief review of the last one hundred years or so, shows that young people with difficulties have been supported in many ways, but that more and more young people are being labelled as having behavioural difficulties every year. So, are we getting better at recognising the signs of behaviour, or is behaviour getting worse? Research would suggest that we are getting better at recognising behaviour problems in young people, but a lack of high quality training can leave staff without the skills they need to support such young people. Around 40% of Newly Qualified Teachers (NQTs) leave the profession within 1 year of becoming qualified. One of the most common reasons teachers leave the profession is due to the behaviour of pupils. This costs the tax payer just under 1 billion pounds per year, yet NQT's only receive two to three hours training in behaviour throughout their qualification. The implementation of high quality training in behaviour management strategies, could go some way towards supporting NQT's in those important first years of teaching.

High quality therapeutic support comes at a price and, with budgets being regularly cut, services are forced to look for the cheapest option. A 'quick fix' approach to behaviour and a lack of training, means that people can sometimes resort to punishments in an attempt to control behaviour, rather than understanding and addressing the underlying cause of the behaviour. Such strategies often serve as a sticking plaster and do little to change the long-term behaviour by teaching the pupil how to behave.

The last 100 years have taught us that we can teach young people to behave in three key ways, by modelling behaviour, teaching alternative behaviours and developing emotional intelligence.

Controlling Behaviour

In the United Kingdom, we sometimes aim to control behaviour through the use of punishments and rewards, even though there is very little evidence to suggest that such approaches are effective in teaching people how to control their own behaviour (Dreikurs and Grey 1972). Punishments can be described as a process delivered after an exhibited behaviour or the act of imposing an aversive or painful stimulus. The purpose of a punishment is to reduce the frequency or intensity with which the behaviour occurs (Lefton 1991), by making the outcome of the behaviour undesirable, the probability of the behaviour occurring again would be reduced. For punishments to be long term effective they would need to be applied every time the behaviour was exhibited which would be difficult to achieve when the young person is outside the environment where the punishment is implemented. In 1948 B.F Skinner explored how punishments can sometimes encourage young people to show a more desirable behaviour, by making the undesirable behaviour undesirable; the idea is that young people should feel better for doing the right thing and eventually change the habitual behaviour. Again, this can have flaws if the punishment is delivered inconsistently. B.F Skinner coined the term 'operant conditioning' when he explored how animals reacted to positive and negative reinforcements. Positive reinforcements occur following a behaviour when an individual is given a consequence that they find rewarding. The aim of positive reinforcement is to increase the likelihood of the behaviour reoccurring. Although Positive reinforcement can be a very powerful way to change behaviour they need to be consistently applied in a range of environments. Failure to consistently apply the strategy can have an adverse effect.

One hundred people were once invited to clean a local park. At the end of the day, fifty of the people were given $10 and told they had worked very hard. One year later the same people were invited back, but it was made clear that no one would receive payment. Interestingly, the only people who turned up to clean the park were the people who did not get paid. The view of the people who got paid initially was that, if they were not going to get paid again, then they were not going to clean the park, even though they had volunteered previously.

Rewarding 'good behaviour' sends a message that young people must be doing something difficult or special; this can make good behaviour less desirable. Whilst such systems have proven to be effective, individuals can become over reliant on the extrinsic reward, making it difficult to adjust when the reward is removed. Many schools use reward systems in some amazing and creative ways and these strategies can be very effective in changing behaviour. However, rewards for behaviour should be individualized and include some mechanism to wean young people off them, failure to do this can sometimes lead to catastrophic outcomes in later life. We might reward a child with a sticker for walking down a corridor, or holding a door open for a member of staff, but we must consider the consequences when we stop rewarding these expectations.

There has been very little research into the long-term impact of rewards on behaviour. One of the most extensive studies was completed by University of East Anglia in 2000. The study found that young people felt the use of gifts was the most effective reward, verbal praise was the least effective. The young people reported that rewards and sanctions did not alter their long-term behaviour. The study also found that in schools where students are motivated by an intrinsic desire to learn, formal rewards systems would be redundant. Interestingly, staff in all the schools that took part in the study reported a lack of consistency in implementing the school's rewards systems. In a school where we removed all the reward systems we saw an increase in low level disruption, the school panicked and wanted to reinstate the systems they had but instead we explored why low level disruption was increased. We concluded that the increase in low level disruption was down to two things.

- Removal of the reward systems that pupils were used to.
- Quality of teaching

Instead of reinstating the reward system the school decided to 'ride the storm' and focus their attention on improving the quality of teaching. The school no longer uses extrinsic rewards and sees low level disruption as an opportunity to adjust the teaching style or address the underlying cause.

Sometimes people mistake negative reinforcement with punishment but these are very different and can have completely different outcomes. In operant conditioning (Skinner 1948) explained that Negative Reinforcements involve the removal of the aversive stimulus to increase the occurring behaviour, because we are removing a stimulus this is known as negative reinforcement. Negative reinforcements should be logically or naturally linked to the behaviour. e.g. Removing a class from the loud noise of a fire alarm or getting children to work in class to remove homework.

> *Negative reinforcement is one of the most consistently misunderstood principles of behaviour.*
>
> Cooper, Heron and Heward (2007)

Where reinforcements strengthen a response, punishments weaken a response. Punishments are designed to make someone feel bad about their behaviour and occur when an aversive consequence that is not linked to the behaviour is implemented.

Although punishments seem rational, we must consider the impact they have on young people. We know that one of the most effective ways to teach a child to behave is to lead by example. I asked over 100 people what was the first thing they did when they saw a speed camera? 85% of the people questioned said that they slowed down; the other 10% said they would check their speed and then slow down. Only 5% of the sample group said that they don't ever speed. When I asked the group what they did once they had passed the speed camera, 78% of the sample group stated that they speed back up again. The purpose of this experiment was to explore how effective speed cameras are at teaching people to control their own behaviour? It is evident that speed cameras control behaviour through the fear punishments such as, paying a fine or getting points on a driving licence, yet the problem with such punishments is that they do little to teach people how to control their own behaviour.

Another problem with punishments is that they only control people within a certain environment e.g. the speed camera can only catch people between the white marks on the road. Like many people, I have been fortunate enough to attend one of those speed awareness courses, a course that is designed to teach someone about speeding, because they have been speeding, is a logical consequence (Dreikurs and Grey 1972), because the consequence is linked to the behaviour.

Research carried out by Professor Robin Martin at Aston University Business School, explored the behaviour of 1311 motorists and concluded that the course improved people's attitudes and intention not to speed and that the benefits of the course occurred immediately.

In 2013 I explored the effect of a common punishment that is used in schools all over the UK, detentions. One school reported that students earned more and more detentions the longer they were at the school and this made the school question the effectiveness of the strategy; this then prompted my study into an alternative approach to detentions in mainstream secondary schools.

Interestingly the example the Oxford Dictionary chooses to put detentions into context is "teachers were divided as to the effectiveness of detention" many staff do feel this way. One reason why schools might support the use of detentions, may be due to schools being unaware of alternative behaviour management strategies, or it might be that schools are unaware of the individual needs of young people.

'Using detention as a 'catch all' cure for student misbehaviours is like using one medicine for every physical ailment'
(Johnson, 2005 p65)

Cotton and Savard (1982) found that punishments such as detentions can be an effective method of controlling individual behaviour and improving school climate. The research suggested that punishment is most effective if it is:

- In proportion with the offence committed
- Perceived by the student as punishment
- Delivered with support.

Although this research states that, for a punishment to be effective it needs to be in proportion to the committed offence. This can be very difficult to implement when we consider that we are all individuals: what might be proportionate for one person may not be for another. A 'clip around the ear' may seem proportionate to some people for any minor misdemeanour, others may disagree. Cotton *et al* stated that punishments should be delivered with support. This view was supported by Van Bockern et al (2008) who suggested that:

The traditional "stay silent, sit still, do nothing" school detention approach is a punitive and ineffective way to change behaviour. It does little to create positive school climates. For children who have been traumatized through fear, isolation, and emotional abuse, poorly managed detention can add to that trauma."

Van Bockern (2008)

Although there is a place for punishments, we must consider that they are aimed at controlling people and do little to teach people how to control their own behaviour. Van Bockern et al (2008) found that punitive approaches do little to create a positive ethos within schools. Although young people in these environments often behave how the staff member wants them to behave, this can sometimes have an adverse impact on individuals, as they may not learn to control their own behaviour, because the underlying issues might not be addressed; these young people can often be involved in many incidents when controlling adults are not present, because punished behaviour is not forgotten, but suppressed and often returns when the punishment is not present.

> *"Within these walls the future may be being forged.*
> *Or maybe Jez is getting trashed on cider.*
> *But when you melt you become the shape of your surroundings.*
> *Your horizons become wider.*
> *Don't they teach you no brains at that school?"*
>
> Jarvis Cocker 'Off The Shelf' 2005

In Victorian times children were put in a corner and made to wear a tall pointed hat with the letter 'D' or the word 'Dunce' on the front which was used as a punishment to humiliate children who 'struggled' or 'misbehaved', to make them think about their behaviour. Naughty chairs have been widely publicised by television shows that show parents how to control children. Such strategies were quickly transferred to the school environment where the name was changed to the thinking chair, or the time out chair, in an attempt to legitimise the technique. Many believe that giving a child timeout in this way, will give the child time to think about their own behaviour, but the technique is aimed at very young children who may not have this understanding yet. Staff in schools should understand that such strategies are designed for parents who may be at home alone with their child and beginning to lose control themselves. Sitting a child somewhere whilst recomposing oneself can be an extremely good strategy, but it does little for the child; this is because children need a secure attachment and they are dependent on parents or carers to meet their basic needs, not having these needs met can have a negative impact on a child.

The use of traffic lights to control young people seems to be common practice in many classrooms. The idea is that all the young people start on the green light and if they do something wrong they are moved to the amber light. If the behaviour continues young people are then moved to the red light. Sunshine and clouds are often used in the same way; the child starts on the sunshine and is moved to the cloud when they show negative behaviour. Some schools write a child's name on the board when they misbehave. These strategies simply control young people through the fear of humiliation and, again do very little to teach young people how to behave. Negative behaviour strategies such as these, can have a profound impact on a child's self-esteem. According to Skinner (1979) these methods are ineffective and young people simply comply to try to avoid the punishment. Some young people who took part in the research felt that punitive behaviour management strategies were ineffective and focused on behaviour, rather than on the feelings driving the behaviour (Long, N. J., Wood, M. M., & Fecser, F. A. 2001). The research in this area is very clear, it is never a good idea to make a child feel humiliated; punishments such as these can often lead to other problems such as depression, increased anxiety and aggression. Smallwood (2010) states: "Humiliation may produce some fear-based behaviour change immediately, but its harm far outweighs any presumed benefits. Humiliation belittles, diminishes, makes smaller. People who experience this kind of toxic atmosphere suffer severe damage". Imagine if we started using these strategies in the staffroom for the teachers who didn't get their planning in on time, or were late for a staff meeting.

Focusing on the underlying cause of the behaviour enables staff to respond more effectively and teaches young people more appropriate ways of expressing their need for support (DfES, 2005). One way we teach young people how to behave is by modelling behaviour (Bandura 1961). During his famous and somewhat controversial 'Bobo doll experiment', Bandura observed young people playing with an inflatable doll. An adult was introduced who behaved aggressively towards the doll. Bandura discovered that young people learn behaviour via observation. If staff model that they can get people to do what they want via the use of punishments, we must also take into consideration what we are teaching others. Often young people do not have the power to put other young people in detention, or the right to take them off the sunshine and put them on a cloud. Young people quickly learn that they need to find other ways to punish young people who have upset them or made them feel angry.

Good behaviour management should have a long-term impact on the individual's behaviour, by teaching the individual how to behave in a variety of environments. Strategies that only work in the environment in which they are used, do very little to support the individual outside that environment.

It is important that, where controlling strategies are implemented, we consider ways to wean individuals off these strategies and promote responsibility; it is important that young people naturally want to improve. Failure to wean young people off rewards can be problematic, because rewards can become relied upon. Young people in year 7 can sometimes have difficulties in secondary schools, due to controlling systems that were put in place in primary education.

I was in a secondary school where a small group of young people refused to enter a maths lesson. When questioned, the young people could not see the benefit of going into the lesson, they explained that they did not get points as they did in their primary school, so they were not motivated to learn maths.

Those who are against punitive behaviour management strategies often turn to extrinsic motivation strategies such as rewards systems, or token economies for behaviour modification. A token economy is a strategy that is based on reinforcing the desired behaviour and ignoring or punishing the undesired behaviour. These strategies have their place and can be very effective; but strategies like this can also dilute intrinsic motivation. Rewards lead to entitlement and young people begin to feel that they should receive a reward for doing what is expected; systems are fraught with problems if used incorrectly and inconsistently.

I took my son to school when he was seven years old and he was keen to show me his reward card that had four stickers on it. He was also keen to tell me that another child in the class had one hundred and twenty stickers on his reward card. I obviously challenged the teacher, who told me not to worry and that she would put some more stickers on my son's card. The next morning, on entering the classroom, my son was promptly praised for 'Good walking' and awarded two stickers. My son explained that he did not walk into the classroom to get a sticker, he walked into the classroom because that's what you are supposed to do.

"I didn't walk into the classroom to get a sticker, I walked into the classroom because that's what you do"
Max Cotton, Age 7

I suppose that rewards and punishments can be a little bit like pain killers, if we are not careful they can mask underlying problems.

Proactive behaviour management responses can be an effective way of controlling an individual's behaviour and can sometimes mean that we rarely see negative behaviour; this is not necessarily a good thing. If an individual is never exposed to negative situations how can they build resilience?

Environment

A good environment is dependent on many factors all working together in harmony. Some contributory factors include the temperature of the room, or the smell of a room; an untidy room can give a negative message to an individual. For individuals with ASD or mental health problems, the colour of the walls can have a negative impact on behaviour or the colour of clothes people are wearing. If too much sensory stimulus is occurring at once people could suffer sensory overload where they might shut down or become aggressive. The location of where individuals sit in the room can also be an important factor for some children this could be due to the light in that particular area or the dynamics with others around them. It is also worth considering the environment that we create personally and professionally. Negative attitudes towards young people, or unrealistic expectations, go a long way towards creating negative environments. Other environmental factors include the layout of the classroom; classroom layout should be practical and allow ease of movement, too much furniture in a room can easily reduce the amount of floor space forcing people to enter intimate space which can result in raised anxieties. For some people music, can play an important part in creating a relaxed atmosphere and help establish a positive learning state that can increase attention, enhance imagination and add an element of fun to the learning environment. When considering the use of music, it is important we consider the type of music and volume of the music. We must consider that some individuals can find it difficult to concentrate when music is playing resulting in negative outcomes. Children's homes and other care settings should carefully consider the environment where the young people live. I strongly believe that homes should be homes but sometimes legislation can get in the way. Some children's homes I visit have fire extinguishers mounted on the walls and Health and Safety at Work Act posters on the walls. Although these are extremely important the homes should take steps to ensure the environment is not too clinical, it is after all a home so it should be as homely as possible. We also need to be very careful when considering the environment for people with attachment disorder, such people may like untidy and unorganised environments which might not fit in with the organisations beliefs. The best environments are those which are supportive, caring and consider the individual needs of the people who attend them.

Learning styles / teaching styles

In school settings, it is important that we consider the learning styles of the young people we are educating, or more accurately our teaching style. In the early 1980s Howard Gardner of Harvard University claimed to have identified 7 distinct types of intelligences:

- Visuo-spatial,
- Musical,
- Bodily-kinaesthetic,
- Interpersonal,
- Linguistic,
- Intrapersonal,
- Logical-mathematical.

Gardners research was hugely successful and widely accepted in education systems around the world. But further research by the likes of Jones *et al.* (2009) suggest that children learn better when presented with information in a way that takes them out of their comfort zone. There is little scientific evidence to show that learning styles have any impact on the amount of information individuals take on-board and they are now seen by many as one of neurosciences greatest myths.

Rather than focus on learning styles we may find it more beneficial to focus on teaching styles, these are typically:

- Formal / Authority, or lecture style
- Demonstrator / personal, or coach style
- Facilitator, or activity style
- Delegator, or group style

Some of the best educators use a blend of teaching styles that focuses on engaging learners in the learning process and helps them develop critical thinking skills. If a pupil struggles in a certain subject, it might not be that the individual does not like the subject, more the style in which the subject is taught.

Expectations

Good proactive support often comes from realistic expectations. Expectations need to be rigorously enforced but setting strict rules can sometimes create problems that might have a detrimental impact on the learning environment. Limits are often seen as a target, for example if the speed limit is 30 mph then that's how fast most people will drive (or faster) but if the speed limit was set at 20 and we drove faster it would almost certainly be slower than 30 mph. One school I supported had a rule that the school tie should always have at least two stripes showing. Most the students within the school had only two stripes showing but most of the students pushed the rule to the limit, showing slightly less than two stripes. If we constantly challenge children for pushing the boundaries we can quite easily create a negative environment and it doesn't take long before children don't like school. It is often more effective to support people who push the boundaries in a low-key way and on an individual basis. If expectations are set too high, people feel negative when the expectations are not met; this can lead to disappointment, which can in-turn, lead to negative behaviour from all parties. Leading by example is also a good way of reinforcing expectations. If pupils are not permitted to wear short skirts, makeup or jewellery should this also be a rule for staff?

Routines

Some of the world's top performers follow routines in order to help them focus on the things they believe to be important. Routine provides a sense of structure and familiarity and teach young people how to control themselves, helping them feel safe and relaxed. Routine helps people to schedule their days, eliminating the need to worry about what is coming next. Children with Autism rely heavily on routines and staff should take steps to ensure the routine is communicated to such individuals appropriately. This can be achieved through visual timetable or now and next boards. Although these strategies were designed specifically for these children I find that most people benefit from them. Routines don't only help children but help staff feel more relaxed and allowing them to focus on the here and now without the uncertainty of what is around the corner. Routines make us more efficient, create structure, build momentum and build self-confidence.

Communication

Behaviour is often a breakdown in communication. Challenging behaviour is an individual's means of expressing a need for support. Young people with communication difficulties might have problems letting people know about their experiences, or how they are feeling. Thorley (2000) found that behavioural difficulties with a medical component, frequently co-occurred with communication difficulty in young children. Heneker (2005) explored the link between behaviour and communication. This study found that 55% - 100% of young people who were

experiencing Behavioural, Emotional and Soc
(BESD) also had some degree of communica
Adults should strive to understand the purpose o
behaviour to best support the individual. I recently witnessed a child with autism throw a chair across a classroom. The child was very quickly removed and allowed to calm. The staff were keen to explain that there was no trigger and he often "kicked off for no reason". Through supporting the child, we quickly learned that it was too hot in the classroom and the child did not have the skills to say "excuse me, it's a little warm in here"; however, the child had learned that, if he threw a chair, he would be removed from the classroom to a cooler place.

Positive Relationships

In his inspiring TED talk in 2015 Robert Waldinger, who is the director of a 75year study into what makes a good life, talked of the importance of positive relationships. Positive relationships have an extremely positive impact on our overall health. Planned responses from staff can help maintain positive relationships with individuals. Trust, respect, shared interests and many other ingredients all help develop positive relationships; however, I trust, respect and have shared interests with people with whom I not have a positive relationship with. In fact, what builds positive relationships are shared positive experiences and shared negative experiences. In a good relationship, the positive experiences should outweigh the negative ones, but we need to understand that shared positive experiences are generally not as powerful as shared negative experiences. It has been said, that negative experiences are seven times more powerful than positive experiences. With this in mind, we need to consider that, for every negative experience we share with someone, we must share at least seven positive experiences to break even.

In the pie chart below, the light area represents shared negative experiences and the dark area represents shared positive experiences, this is a good relationship. If the chart was reversed then, obviously, this would be a poor relationship.

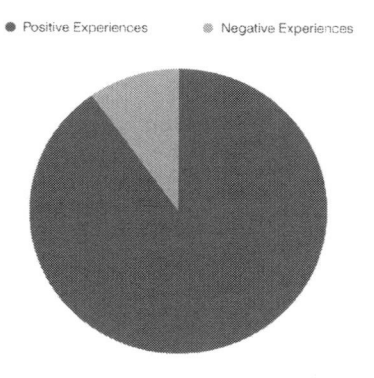

It is important to note that, shared negative experiences do not always damage relationships, negative experiences can often bring people closer together, if neither party instigated the negative experience. Another factor to consider is that negative experiences can often be turned into positive experience through Post Incident Learning and Support (PILS), on the premise that learning from an experience is a positive outcome and we learn more from mistakes than we do successes.

If you imagine young people walking around with a piggy bank, when someone shouts at a child or humiliates a child, we withdraw £7, but when we share a positive experience with a child, we only put £1 in the piggy bank. All this is very subjective, but following this rule can help adults build positive relationships with young people: one of the contributory factors to good behaviour management.

Focusing on Behaviour

To promote positive behaviour, we must start with a belief. Research shows that our beliefs influence our behaviour. If I believe that I cannot do something, the chance of me doing it is dramatically reduced, when we genuinely believe we can achieve our chances of success are far greater. In the famous and very controversial 'blue eyes, brown eye' experiment of 1968, Jane Elliott who was a third-grade teacher wanted to demonstrate to her class the importance of equality after one of her 9-year-old students 'jokingly' told her that he shot Martin Luther King. Jane Elliott asked her class if they would find it interesting to judge people by the colour of their eyes and split her class of nine and ten year olds into those with brown eyes and those with blue eyes. Since Jane Elliott had blue eyes, she decided that the blue-eyed children should be on top and the brown-eyed children were made to wear collars, so that they could be easily recognised. The children with brown eyes were treated like second-class citizens for the day and the blue-eyed children were given rewards, such as extra playtime, in addition the blue eyed children were not allowed to play with the brown-eyed children; the following day the roles were reversed. During the experiment, the children were tested using a card-pack: the children wearing the collars did not do as well as they did when they were not wearing the collars, on both days. What this experiment showed was that people often live up to expectation and, if we believe that we are not as good as others, we probably will not be.

'Treat people as if they were what they ought to be, and you help them to become what they are capable of being

Johann Wolfgang von Goethe

Beliefs play a huge part of behaviour management and it is important that negative beliefs are challenged because they are all too often damaging. Negative beliefs can be changed to positive beliefs, by giving the individual with the negative belief, different experiences. I used to think that Coldplay were a good band, so my wife bought me tickets to see them live. The concert was amazing and I came away thinking that Coldplay were one of the best bands in the world. The experience had changed my belief from thinking that the band was good to, they were one of the best bands in the world. When a new Coldplay album was released, I download my copy and listened to it on my way home from a Conference. By the time I had got home, I had convinced myself that Coldplay were rubbish and I had changed my beliefs again.

The term 'behavioural problems' can sometimes encourage staff to focus on the negative behaviour of an individual and after a few hours' staff strongly believe that the individual has behaviour problems, this is known as selective attention which will be explored later in this chapter. When I asked staff in a variety of service settings what the challenging behaviours are that individuals show, the most severe behaviours are generally ones like, "He throws chairs and attacks staff". This is often described as 'Kicking Off'. The term "Kick off" can be dangerous and does little to create a supportive environment. I am often asked to support schools where young people often "kick off"! The impression this message creates is one of chaos where young people are out of control. Interestingly, when I am asked to support schools where young people often "need support," this language seems to creates a much more positive impression and I usually find these settings are much more supportive than those where children "kick off". Changing the language, we use (even in the staff room) can go some way towards creating a more positive environment. This is much more than just a play on words, the term 'kick off' encourages staff to focus on high-level behaviour, missing the more important and much easier to manage low-level behaviours, where early intervention may be enough to support the individual.

What can you see on the next page of this book?

●

Some people see a dot? Some people see a dot on a page, others see an aerial shot of a person wearing a large sombrero, but what else can you see? What about the header at the top of the page? What about your hands holding this book? Your thumbnails? A cup of coffee on the desk in the background or a large glass of wine?

The dot on the previous page might represent behaviour and, if we focus on the behaviour, we stand very little chance of changing it; we need to look beyond the behaviour. It is fascinating how people often focus on the behaviour of young people, but we do not seem to do this much with adults. I often ask staff working in schools, what their response might be if an angry student walked into a classroom and knocked a chair over in temper. Staff often respond with "I would tell them to pick the chair up" or "to get out of the classroom". I wonder what their response would be if an angry member of staff walked into the staffroom and knocked over a chair in temper? The good people amongst us would probably respond with "Are you alright? What's happened? Do you want to talk about it?" When a child shows challenging behaviour, we often focus on the behaviour itself, but with adults, we tend to focus more on what is driving the behaviour. Focusing on the roots of the behaviour puts us in a much better place to address the behaviour.

When we are told that a young person presents challenging behaviour, we start to focus on the behaviour and we almost wait for the young person to show the negative behaviour, this is known as selective attention. Without looking at your watch, can you describe it? Does it have numbers, roman numerals or lines to represent the numbers? What colour is the watch face and what colour are the hands? Many people cannot describe their watch even though they might look at it 10 to 20 times per day, this is because when we look at our watches we focus on the time and miss the detail.

One other problem with focusing on behaviour is that different behaviours sometimes get very different response for example, if a child self-harms they get support, whereas if a child hurts others they often get punished.

In conclusion, when a child behaves in a certain way, staff should aim to understand the functionality of the behaviour; in this way staff, would be better placed to put supportive strategies in place.

Teaching Behaviour

If we want to change behaviour it is important that we understand where behaviour comes from. Everyone has had a huge variety of experiences in their life and it is these experiences that shape how we feel. Our experiences and feelings shape how we behave.

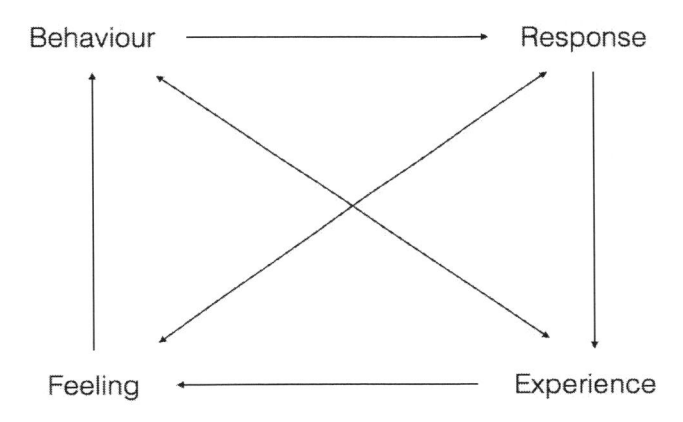

```
Behaviour  ─────────────▶  Response
    ▲  ╲              ╱  ▲
    │    ╲          ╱    │
    │      ╲      ╱      │
    │        ╲  ╱        │
    │        ╱  ╲        │
    │      ╱      ╲      │
    │    ╱          ╲    │
    │  ╱              ╲  ▼
Feeling  ◀─────────────  Experience
```

Experiences we have do not need to be real experiences, they can also be imagined. I still get a little anxious around Jammy Dodger biscuits because of a recurring dream I had when I was a child where I was chased by masses of Jammy dodgers. The dream I had was a negative experience and this in turn drives feelings of anxiety when I see the biscuits, I still like the taste of them though! Negative experience can often drive negative feelings; negative feelings can often drive what we think of as negative behaviour. The negative behaviour from a child might be a negative experience for the adults, which can drive negative feelings, which in turn drives negative behaviour from the adult such as shouting at the child. This gives the child another negative experience and the cycle starts again. Of course, it is often not quite as simple as that because sometimes feelings might drive an experience. If we feel good about something we might want to repeat the experience. Sometimes behaving in a certain way might create certain feelings. In fact, experiences, feelings and behaviours all interact with each other. It's also important to understand that it doesn't always work in this way, sometimes a negative feeling can drive positive behaviour especially if we learn something because of the experience / feeling, for example if I touch something hot (experience), I might feel pain (negative feeling), this might drive more positive behaviour if I learn not to touch it again, this is what is known as a natural consequence and is a very powerful behaviour modification strategy. Natural consequences will be discussed later in this book.

We know that negative behaviour management strategies such as punishments can drive negative feelings that in turn can often drive more negative behaviour, such strategies do little to create positive environments and positive relationships therefore such strategies can have a negative impact on behaviour.

As an adult working in a school and/or other service setting, we have a duty of care, so it is our job to aim to break this cycle. To break the cycle, we need to change any one of the contributory factors, i.e. the experience, feeling or behaviour. Changing anyone of these factors is likely to result in a different outcome.

Change the experience

We cannot change experience that individuals have had, but we can certainly change how we see them, for example if a child has had a negative experience around adults, we can give them positive experiences around us. If a child has had a negative experience in school, we can aim to ensure they have positive experiences in school.

When I was 7 years old my teacher publicly humiliated me. I had made a Christmas card using a variety of media (as per the instructions). I wanted to write 'Happy Christmas,' but I didn't know how to spell Christmas, so I went to ask the teacher. The teacher told me to sit down and use my initiative. I returned to my desk confused because I thought that asking the teacher was using my initiative. I thought for a while and then decided to go and get a dictionary; halfway across the classroom the teacher shouted, "Cotton sit down!" I tried to explain that I was going to get a dictionary, but was told again to sit down. After giving this some thought I decided that I would ask another child. When you are 7 years old, if you want to ask someone how to spell something, you ask the best speller. Ian was the best speller, so I thought I would ask him. The problem was that Ian was sat over the other side of the classroom. I shouted "IAN!" under my breath, but he didn't hear me. I tried again a little louder, but he still didn't hear me. The third time was quite a lot louder and this time he heard me, but so did the teacher. "Stop disturbing other pupils Cotton and get on with your work!" she shouted. When the teacher told me not to disturb 'other' pupils, that's what I thought she meant, I didn't understand that this also meant Ian. I thought of many ways to get his attention without disturbing other pupils and decided that I would throw my rubber at him. It was a perfect shot and the rubber hit Ian on his neck. Ian turned and glared at me, then threw his hand in the air and said "Miss! Cotton's just thrown a rubber at me!" The teacher was extremely angry now and told me that I had one last chance, "either get on with your work or get out of the classroom!" she yelled. I sat there wondering how I could 'use my initiative' to work out how to spell Christmas? Then it came to me, I would spell Christmas the short way. At 7 years old I would get some letters mixed up (like other 7 year old children). Instead of writing 'Happy Xmas' on my card, I wrote 'Happy Zmas'. I took the card to my teacher and, on the way, I looked at all the other cards the children were making, I couldn't believe it, mine was the best and I had finished first. I placed the card in front of the teacher and said "I've finished" The teacher took the card by the corner with her index finger and thumb, she looked at it, pulled a face and slammed my card down on the table. The teacher held up her hand and shouted "Everyone, stop what you are doing, look this way and listen!" The classroom fell silent; the teacher then picked up my card and said "Dean didn't know how to spell Christmas, so he put Zmas!" Of course, everyone began to laugh and I was totally humiliated.

That experience shaped my negative feelings about school, but 12 years later I walked into Reignhead School in Sheffield to deliver a parcel and my negative experience of school was changed immediately.

Change the feeling

Growing understanding of the brain, shows constant interaction between emotions and physical state (Faupel et al 1998), this emphasis on emotions goes back to Freud (1923) whose early work around Psychodynamics studied the theory that psychological forces underlie human behaviour. Although Freud's work is recognised historically but was downgraded in scientific study, his work emphasizes the interaction between unconscious and conscious motivation and the significance of emotions. Social and Emotional Aspects of Learning (SEAL) (DfES, 2005) encourages staff to focus on the underlying causes of difficult behaviour and suggests that concentrating on feelings, rather than behavioural outcomes enables staff to respond more effectively. Young people learn to enhance their self-awareness which allows them to manage their feelings more effectively and develop a wider range of responses. Changing how we see things can change how we feel about things. It can be difficult to change how people feel about things without changing the experience, however, developing a child's emotional literacy can help us recognize how the child feels. If you ask a 3-year-old child how they are feeling, you generally get one of two common answers. 'Happy or Sad'. The way we support an individual who is stressed, might be very different to how you might support an individual who is feeling upset, for example if someone is stressed, you might give them space, but if someone is feeling upset, you might give them a hug. When discussing feeling with individuals we should also explore the intensity of the feeling. We are likely to get different behaviour if someone is feeling a little upset and extremely upset so it is also important that we explore the intensity of feeling.

We know that we can teach behaviour through modelling appropriate behaviour but sometimes we can miss some great opportunities to demonstrate appropriate behaviour and hide our feelings from children. If you have had a bad morning, maybe you had an argument with your partner, a flat tyre on the way to work and it is raining heavily. Some staff put their professional hat on the moment they walk into the service, missing an opportunity to tell children how they are feeling and how they are dealing with it.

By developing emotional intelligence, we can fine-tune our responses to feelings in order to gain a more accurate outcome. The emotional assessment tool on the following page was developed by Ledson and Moffat in 2010, in an attempt to support staff in assessing the emotional intelligence of young people in their service. Ledson and Moffat found the assessment tool helped to structure accurate, individualised support for young people with Autistic spectrum disorder.

HOW TO TEACH BEHAVIOUR AND HOW NOT TO

		Happy	Sad	Excited	Bored	Anxious	Relief	Angry	Calm	Scared	Safe	Love	Hate	Keen	Tired	Proud	Shame	Envy / Jealousy	Guilty	Satisfaction	Pain	Pleasure	Relaxed	Stressed	Frustrated	Confused	Understanding	Empathy
Symbols	Look at symbol of emotion at any time																											
	Identify symbol of emotion at any time																											
	Look at symbol of emotion when experiencing the emotion																											
	identify the symbol of emotion when experiencing the emotion																											
Photographs	Look at photo of emotion at any time																											
	identify photo of emotion at any time																											
	Look at photo of emotion when experiencing the emotion																											
	Identify the photo of emotion when experiencing the emotion																											
Others	Look at another person (not picture) who is experiencing an emotion																											
	Identify the emotion a person (not picture) is experiencing using symbols to support																											
	Identify the emotion a person (not picture) is experiencing using no symbols																											
Themselves	Respond to "You are feeling….?" for positive emotions using symbols to support while they are experiencing the emotion																											
	Respond to "You are feeling….?" for negative emotions using symbols to support while they are experiencing the emotion																											
	Respond to "You are feeling….?" for positive emotions using no symbols while they are experiencing the emotion																											
	Respond to "You are feeling….?" for negative emotions using no symbols while they are experiencing the emotion																											
	Inform others of how they are feeling (positive emotions) without being asked while they are experiencing the emotion using symbols as support																											
	Inform others of how they are feeling (positive emotions) without being asked while they are experiencing the emotion using no symbols																											
	Inform others of how they are feeling (negative emotions) without being asked while they are experiencing the emotion using symbols as support																											
	Inform others of how they are feeling (negative emotions) without being asked while they are experiencing the emotion using no symbols																											
	Inform others of how they are feeling (negative emotions) without being asked while they are experiencing the emotion using no symbols and manage their feelings appropriately with support																											
	Inform others of how they are feeling (negative emotions) without being asked while they are experiencing the emotion using no symbols and manage their feelings appropriately with no support																											

Change the Behaviour / Response

To change behaviour, it is important that we know what behaviour we want to see, in place of the behaviour we are seeing. The three questions below can help focus staff to support young people and help them change.

- What is the behaviour we want to change?
- What is the opposite positive behaviour we want to see instead?
- How do we teach the behaviour we want to see?

For example, if a child continually calls out in class. The opposite positive behaviour would be making themselves heard appropriately which might be putting their hand up? We could just tell the pupil to put their hand up but that might not be very effective? A more effective method would be to talk to the child and ask them how they could gain attention in a more appropriate way and then practice the selected strategy. This simple method can be a very effective strategy for a vast array of behaviours, the key being that we must know what behaviour we want to see in place of the behaviour we don't want to see and then we can focus on teaching the behaviour instead of just telling an individual not to do something.

Some very simple behaviour management strategies can be used to achieve behaviour change. One simple strategy is to tell the individual what you want them to do and not what you do not want them to do. For example, if a pupil is running down a corridor, instead of saying "Don't Run!" a better response would be "Walk, thank you". It is often much better to say "thank you" rather than "please".

> *"I can't change the direction of the wind, but I can adjust my sails to always reach my destination"*
> *Jimmy Dean*

All the above is based on changing the child's experiences, feeling and behaviour, but it is much easier for us to change our own behaviour.

We know that, changing our negative behaviour to more positive behaviour, will give the child a positive experience, that will ultimately drive more positive behaviour. One problem is that staff behaviours are also based on their own experiences and feelings, which can sometimes be negative. A child who makes constant noises may irritate the adult, giving the adult a negative experience resulting in negative reactions. This is where planned reactions from staff can be very effective, especially if the planned reactions are developed by a team of people and not individuals. Plans go a long way towards creating consistency for individuals and ensure that staff give a considered reaction, when faced with a known behaviour. If an adult has a plan then they just need to follow it, this can reduce the stress they might be feeling because they don't have to think on their feet but also plans aid consistency and we know that consistence is often the key to behaviour issues.

A good behaviour policy and strong leadership can create a positive environment for staff and young people. Good policies should be considered as an instruction manual for staff. I find it astonishing how many staff in some schools I support, do not know what is in the school's behaviour policy. Staff in schools are not paid to base their behaviour on their own feelings, they are paid to follow the school's policy. I do not think that staff in other industries could get away with this, for example, If I was a bus driver and the manager told me that I had to drive route number 85, but I didn't like that route and decided that I know a few short cuts, or I wanted to take a more scenic route, I'm sure it wouldn't be long until I was sacked.

If a policy states that staff should follow a behaviour plan when dealing with a certain behaviour, then that is what they need to do. By having a simple plan in place, that is developed by a team of people including the parents/carers and the children themselves (where appropriate), staff can use planned responses when faced with a potentially difficult situation. Plans need to be broken down into stages of arousal and focus on what support staff should give at each stage.

In 2010 I studied talking therapies such as Cognitive Behaviour Therapy (CBT), Counselling, Life Space Interviews (LSI), Life Space Crisis Interviews (LSCI) and many more. During this research, I found that most talking therapies focus on experiences, feelings, behaviours and/or other people's responses. To get access to talking therapies' individuals often need to have already developed a mental health problem and then the experiences, feelings, behaviours and/or other people's responses are explored in detail in a bid to get the individual being supported to see things differently. If we explored the experiences, feelings, behaviours and/or other people's responses following incidents through Post Incident Learning (PIL) then maybe the individual might never develop a mental health condition because they are being supported at source.

Arousal Spectrum

The brain can go through many stages of arousal before it reaches peak aggression, this can be displayed through a spectrum of severity. This ranges from low-level anxiety behaviours, such as tapping or fidgeting to high-level crisis behaviours, such as attacking people, damaging property and depression behaviours, such as being withdrawn and/or upset.

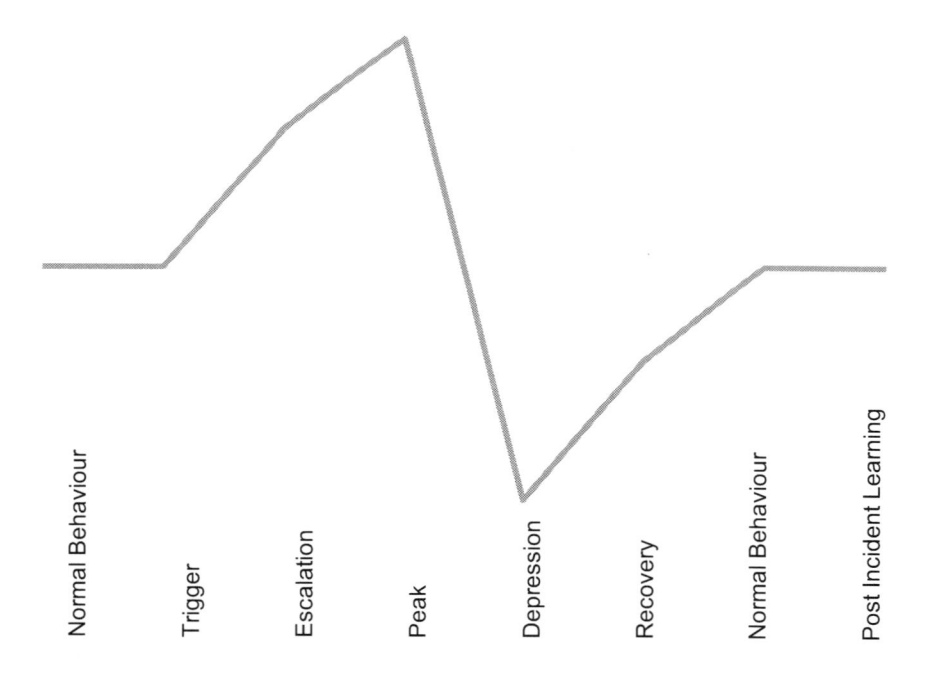

When people are relaxed so is their brain, a relaxed brain is open for learning and there is lots of room to store information and make calculated decisions, for the purpose of this illustration we shall call this 'normal behaviour'. Following a trigger the brain can enter the escalation stage and it begins to close down, rational decisions become more difficult and the information storage space of the brain is reduced. During peak behaviour, when the brain is high on the arousal spectrum it can be extremely difficult for individuals to make rational decisions and there is very little space to store new information. Following 'Peak' the brain gradually begins to relax again; this can cause the individual to become upset or feel depressed. It is important to note that at this stage the brain is still in a high arousal state and individuals often need support.

Normal Behaviour

When developing a behaviour management plan, it is important that all key parties who have a shared interest in the child, have input into the behaviour plan; it is also important that people understand what is the child's 'normal behaviour' and what this looks like. I am often asked to offer advice on how to support young children with 'behaviour problems'. Observations on such children often show no such 'behaviour problems', just 'normal behaviour' of a neurologically typical child of that age. To understand what is 'normal behaviour' for an individual, we need to understand the background of the individual. Young people are sometimes chastised for poor table manners, when the young people may not have been taught table manners at home, or may not have a table to practice on.

Triggers

There is always a trigger for behaviour, but these can often be difficult to recognise due to the complexity of individuals. Triggers can be internal or external, can be based on several experiences and feelings, or an isolated experience. When we are feeling tired or hungry, we might find that we are less tolerant, therefore the trigger would be an internal trigger driven by feelings and moods. An external trigger might arise from an external influence such as somebody saying "no", or another person challenging you in an aggressive way.

Staff often explain that "There are no triggers," or "He just kicked off for no reason", but we all know that this is not true, so why do we say it? One reason is that we understand that a child has a problem and this is just another part of their behaviour. I suppose it can also be easier for an adult to blame the child, rather than admit a lack of understanding around the initial trigger, as sometimes triggers can be difficult to recognise. Another misconception is that we should avoid triggers but this can be problematic. One school I supported cared for a child with autism who attacked staff who wore red. The staff were informed that they were not allowed to wear anything red because they were likely to be attacked. Although safety is paramount the staff in the school had to do a lot of work with this pupil to almost desensitise him and address the underlying course of the behaviour. Informing staff not to wear red would result in the behaviour merely being controlled.

Escalation Behaviour

During the escalation phase, individuals might become increasingly upset or unfocused, exhibit avoidance behaviours, become defensive and may challenge adult authority. When we talk of defensive behaviour, we are generally discussing behaviour that is driven by emotions rather than thought. These defensive behaviours are hard wired into the brain to help shield us from painful feelings.

"To be defensive is to react with a war mentality to a non-war issue."

Sharon Ellison

Another characteristic of the escalation phase is that the rational prefrontal lobes begin to shut down and the reflexive back areas of the brain take over. When the prefrontal lobes shut down, people often make rash decisions and can often give off negative signals. These signals can be seen as negative behaviours, which can often get negative responses and, before we know it, we are at the peak of our behaviour.

Peak Behaviour

Peak behaviour is individualised, as are other behaviours on the spectrum. When entering the peak behaviour stage blood rushes through the frontal cortex, this can have an impact on the individuals rational thought. The adrenal glands saturate the system with the stress hormones adrenaline and cortisol, giving individuals higher levels of energy and strength. This leads to increased blood pressure and heart rate. Peak behaviours may involve shouting at someone, or walking away, but some individual's peak behaviours might involve putting themselves or others at risk of injury or worse. Clearly these behaviours are not socially acceptable in most cultures and in many cases, dangerous. If individuals in our care are hurting themselves or others staff have a duty of care and may need to physically control the individual to keep them safe. Staff in services where these behaviours are exhibited should be trained to support these individuals. For physical restraint to be effective it should be used alongside other behaviour management techniques with an emphasis on diversion, diffusion and de-escalation strategies and learning from the incident.

The key legal words to be considered when considering seclusion and/or physical restraint are:

- Best interest
- Reasonable
- Necessary
- Proportionate.

The 'Best Interest' of the individual in care should always be paramount.

'Reasonable' suggests that staff have carried out a planned or dynamic risk assessment and weighed up the risk. We have decided that the risk of our intervention outweighs the risk of not intervening. Where the risk is unforeseeable seclusion might be considered as part of a dynamic risk assessment. Some argue that seclusion is used as part of a continuum of restrictive physical interventions, if this is the case the psychological impact of the interventions and the restriction and deprivation of liberty should be considered. If seclusion is to be planned for a mental health assessment should be conducted under the 2015 Mental Health Code of Practice.

For something to be 'Necessary' all other behaviour strategies should be exhausted (other than in an emergency for something that was unforeseeable). If service settings have a room which is used for seclusion this suggest that it is not an unforeseeable risk but a foreseeable risk. Therefore, the premise of unforeseeable could be invalid.

There are many training packages in the use of restraint and, although many of them seem very similar, they vary widely (Deveau *et al* 2009).

In 2010 I studied the impact of training staff in physical interventions alongside diversion, diffusion and de-escalation strategies (Cotton 2010), the study found that the training lead to a reduction in behaviour incidents in most cases. It is important to note that it is feelings that drive peak behaviour and managing these feelings is the desired outcome, not suppressing the feelings; in other words, it is ok to feel that way.

When considering the use of Physical Intervention, it is important that we understand that such a technique is only a means of control if used in isolation. In the absence of Post Incident Learning, Physical Intervention merely controls the behaviour and does not teach individuals to control their own behaviour. In some cases, Physical intervention can be counterproductive and increase the risk of dangerous behaviours, especially if young people learn that they can put themselves in danger because staff will intervene and keep them safe.

Depression

Following peak behaviour Individuals in the depression phase can easily loop back into peak behaviours, if they are not given the right support following peak behaviour. Individuals may be in shock or denial and be cut off from their feelings, so they might act as if nothing has happened but they might have feelings of anger or guilt. If an adult is unaware that the individual has exhibited peak behaviours, depression behaviours can be mistaken for escalation behaviours. It is important to note that behaviour strategies to support the individual during the escalation stage, might not be effective in supporting the individual during the depression stage, for example, touch might be effective during the escalation stage, but may loop the individual back to peak behaviour in the depression stage, or vice versa.

The key to understanding what an individual's behaviour looks like at each phase, is to understand the individual. Building positive relationships with others goes a long way towards being able to recognise where they are on the aggression spectrum; and, what supportive strategies can be put in place to help the individual. When I am feeling anxious, I move my legs from side to side, telling me to keep my legs still, doesn't help (as we know this is focusing on the behaviour), if I am told to do this enough, I can re-enter the escalation phase.

During the arousal spectrum, people may lack rational thought. Rational thought or reasoning helps us to understand problems and how to solve them. One problem with rational thought is that it is usually based on our own personal experiences, this is often referred to as, cognitive biases. During our lifetime, we are given lots of information, some of which is useful and some of which is not. We need look no further than Facebook to understand this. I have met many staff that work with very young children who are convinced that they are not allowed to sing "Baa Baa Black Sheep" because it is racist. This lead to staff in nurseries all over the UK singing "Baa Baa Rainbow Sheep", which some might argue to be homophobic. The problem is that rational thought can be unreliable (Tversky and Kahneman 1989), so it is important that teams of people are involved in decision-making and develop plans to support behaviour.

Due to cognitive biases, staff can easily fall into the trap of doing what they feel best, all be it, with good intentions. Plans can help ensure a consistent approach, especially if they are child centred and involve key partners. The 'My Plan' shown in appendix 1, is a simple behaviour plan that I developed which explores some key areas of behaviour and how best to support the individual. A good behaviour plan should explain what the individual's behaviour looks like at each phase of aggression; explore possible strategies for the pupil to use when they are on the arousal spectrum; and ideas of how staff can best support the individual. A good behaviour plan should also explore what the individual enjoys;

provide a list of common de-escalation strategies; plus, information on how best to support the individual following an incident. It is important that the child has ownership of the behaviour plan where possible

Below is a description of the de-escalation techniques on the 'My Plan'. The success of all de-escalation techniques often depends on the person using the techniques and the relationship they have with the individual.

Verbal advice and support,

Giving someone verbal advice and support involves much more than the words that come out of your mouth. Being non-judgmental in how you speak and using positive body language are key contributory factors in using this strategy.

Giving space

Personal space is the area around a person that they regard as their own space, it can be described as a bubble. This space is unique to the individual and is based on many factors, including their own personal experiences. Factors that influence how close you can get to someone include age, gender, race, height, culture to name but a few. The main factors to consider when considering space is the relationship you have with the person and their emotional state. People with a good relationship can often get closer to others without raising anxieties, however, people on the arousal spectrum often have amplified feelings so might need a little more space than usual. Enter the space and you could be entering the 'bubble of trouble'.

Reassurance

Reassuring someone is much more than *telling* them that they are going to be alright and more to do with making them *believe* that they are going to be alright, which removes any doubts or fears. Again, when using reassurance as a de-escalation technique, we must consider the tone of our voice and our body language.

Scripts

Scripts are widely used as an effective de-escalation technique. On calling emergency services, the person on the other end of the line that is very calm. These people receive in-depth training in communication skills and the use of scripts. Scripts are also widely used in call centres and customer services. On Christmas Eve 1999, I bought my Nan a vase (I know there is a lesson there), when I got home I started to wrap the presents and noticed that the vase was damaged. As this was my Nan's Christmas present, I drove back to Meadowhall Shopping Centre to get a replacement. The roads in Sheffield on Christmas Eve were extremely busy and it took me one hour to drive around 5 miles. When I got to the shop, I was feeling extremely angry and frustrated and said to the shop assistant that I felt it was disgusting that I had to waste time on Christmas Eve taking something back. The shop assistant replied, "You're absolutely right, I'll get you another one". When the shop assistant returned, she said how nice she thought the vase was and asked me if I would like another carrier bag (they were free in those days). I left the shop happy, but quickly realized that I had gone from being angry to happy in a very short space of time. Working with young people experiencing social, emotional and behavioural difficulties, I wanted to know how the shop assistant had calmed me down so quickly, so I returned to customer services and asked her how she had done this. To my surprise the shop assistant explained that it was just a script and they used it with everyone. This made me angry again, but also made me realize that I might be able to use this strategy with the young people I worked with. Upon my return to work, I was faced with an angry child who told me how much he hated school, "You're right, I'll get you another one", I replied, but it didn't work, it did, however, make me think about the power of scripts. A set of pre-planned, positive words can help staff to support young people when faced with difficult situations.

Negotiation

Win-Win negotiation can be a powerful tool when de-escalating situations. A Win-Win leaves both parties feeling happy with the result, this helps maintain positive relationships following the incident. Negotiation can be a difficult method to de-escalate a situation, if the individual is high on the arousal spectrum.

Limited Choices

Open choices can often lead to undesirable behaviour from the pupil for example, if we gave a child the choice to get on with their work or get out of the classroom, most staff would not be happy if the pupil took the second choice. Limited choice involves giving the individual only two or three choices, but only choices we would be happy with. Choices can sometimes be manipulated to get a child to take the choice we want them to take. Very young children often take the last choice you give them. The key to choices is to give two choices that both have a positive outcome for example, if I child refuses to do some work, we could ask the child if they would prefer to do the work in a few minutes or now? I would rather offer these choices than tell the child that they can either do it now or after school. Young people often show negative behaviour because they don't know what else to do. Using choices in this way can help teach the child that there are better ways. To increase the likelihood of the child choosing the preferred response, distraction can be used, whilst giving the choices. If I put a red and blue pen on a table and asked an individual to pick up the red or blue pen, there is a slightly better chance that the blue pen would be chosen, because blue was said last. However, if I asked an individual to pick up the red pen or the blue pen and then I distracted the individual, the chance of them picking the blue pen increases dramatically. Of course, this method does not take into account other factors? Living in Sheffield the colour of the pen selected depends on whether you support Sheffield United or Sheffield Wednesday; I have yet to see a Sheffield United fan opt for the blue pen, but at least they picked one up.

Humour

Humour can be a great de-escalation technique that can relax young people and build positive relationships, but needs to be used with care. Humour can often be confused with sarcasm and, where humour requires skill and can de-escalate, sarcasm requires little skill and is likely to escalate. Humour can be a very useful proactive, behaviour management technique and is one of the top five qualities that young people like in a teacher.

Tactical ignoring

Planned or tactical ignoring involves ignoring low-level behaviours. If you want something to grow you need to feed it and, if the purpose of the negative behaviour is attention, then giving the attention might feed the behaviour. Although tactical ignoring can be effective and requires little planning, it should not be used as an excuse to do nothing.

Take up time

If a child threw a pen on the floor, we could say "pick that pen up", stand over the child and wait for them to pick the pen up: we could be in for a long wait; or the child may not pick the pen up and we could lose face in front of the entire class. The point is that people need time to think, 'take up time' gives young people the time they need to assess the situation and come to their own conclusion. In take up time, the adult would say, "pick the pen up, thanks" and then continue with whatever it is they were doing. It might take the child a while to pick the pen up, but when they do, the staff should acknowledge that the child did what they were asked: this could be a simple "thanks". Take up time can be even more effective if used in conjunction with limited choices for example, do you want to pick the pen up in a few minutes or now? Thanks!

Time-out / Time-in

'Time-out' can take many forms and people describe 'Time-out' in many ways, from sitting a child on a 'naughty step', to forcing them to spend time alone, against their will, (which normally requires statutory powers). For me, 'Time-out' means removing positive reinforcements that might be fuelling the behaviour; it should not be used as a punishment. (Siegal & Bryson 2014) explained that 'Time- out' can neurobiologically damage young people. Ideally, young people should take themselves to time out, to give themselves a chance to self-regulate. We have already discussed a child's need for secure attachment, so time-outs do little to teach appropriate behaviour, unless they are accompanied with a post incident learning (PILS) structure, this is known as 'Time-in'.

Supportive touch

Supportive touch should be used with care, but it is a very powerful behaviour management technique, especially if used as part of pedagogy. It is considered appropriate, in most cultures, to touch between shoulder and elbow. We can use touch when acknowledging behaviour we want to see or to re-focus a young person when they are distracted. One thing to consider when using touch is the difference between light pressure and deep pressure touch. Light pressure touch stimulates, whereas deep pressure touch lowers the blood pressure and relaxes. If supportive touch is to be used, we need a good understanding of where that individual is on the arousal spectrum. Supportive touch can work well in the depression phase, but can sometimes escalate behaviours if used in the escalation stage. The key, when using supportive touch, is the relationship we have with the individuals we are using the technique with.

Transfer adult / staff

Aggression is often focused at the first person on the scene, so allowing another adult to take over the management of a potentially aggressive situation, can be a very effective de-escalation technique. Staff should not see the transfer of staff as a weakness in their own de-escalation techniques, because roles could quite easily be reversed. If the transfer of staff is used, it is important that the member of staff who left the situation can rebuild the relationship with the other individual involved. It is also important that this approach is non-hierarchical and not overused; calling for someone in a higher position on a regular basis, can often give a message that you cannot cope with the behaviour. It is also a good idea for staff to develop 'secret' scripts for taking over situations. I have visited many services that have been very inventive with scripts like, "There is a telephone call for you" and "Just check on the squirrels in the garden, thanks". "There is a telephone call for you", in this case meant that the person involved in the situation could reply "its ok I'll call them back", but "Just check on the squirrels in the garden, thanks", meant that the person saying the script was going to take over the situation. This was used when the person entering the situation knew more about the situation than the person dealing with it; or the person dealing with the situation was not aware that they were using negative strategies. Although I found this script a little comedic, it seemed to work for the service. Whatever script we decide on should be made clear to staff and included in service settings policy.

Success reminded

When reminding individuals of success, it is important that it is not done in a way that is over the top and false. Success reminders should be subtle, or they may have a negative outcome if the individual believes that you are using the strategy to pre-empt negative behaviour.

Listening

Active listening is where people make a conscious effort to listen, but listening is not the same as hearing. When I was 18 I worked behind a bar and one Saturday afternoon a customer approached and placed her carrier bag of shopping on the bar. The customers purse was in the bottom of her carrier bag so she emptied the shopping on the bar to retrieve her money from the bottom of the bag, in amongst the shopping I spotted two fresh cream and jam scones. The customer found her purse and took out one pound and then asked for some change for the jukebox, I got the change from the till and upon my return I took another longing look at the scones and the customer asked "is the jukebox on?", I thought she said "Would you like a scone" to which I replied yes please, I took the packet, opened it up and tucked into a delicious fresh cream and jam scone. It was only when I had eaten half the scone that I realised that she had not asked me if I wanted a scone!

Listening is about paying attention and trying to understand what is being said, along with trying to understand the unsaid. This involves reading the body language of the speaker and listening to the tone as well as the intonation of what is being said. "I AM FINE!!" whilst making a fist, is different to "I'm fine", said in a calm controlled way. Good listeners have a very high level of self-awareness and are very aware of their own body language. Good body language, when listening, should include mirroring body language, nodding, non-verbal utterances and open body language.

Another very powerful tool that is used by good listeners is that of paraphrasing. Paraphrasing involves the listener repeating what has been said, using different words to check accuracy and allow reflection. When the speaker has finished speaking, checking the key points of the whole dialogue can be a great way to gaining clarity for both the listener and the speaker, this is known as summarising.

Removing audience

An audience can often add fuel to a potential situation just by being in the immediate vicinity, however, the audience can be part of the problem instead of the solution. Take a fight situation for example, we can often tell when there is a fight in a school, because of the crowd of people on the school field. What would happen if the crowd dispersed and left the young people who were going to fight? Often this would be the end of the fight.

Apologising

Apologising as a de-escalation tool is not about making young people say "Sorry". Sometimes staff try to force children into saying sorry, this can sometimes lead to young people saying "SORRY!!!" in a way that suggests that they are not really. This often leads to staff using phrases such as "Not like that!" or "Say it like you mean it!". In some cases, this becomes a huge issue and staff sometimes focus on the apology rather than the primary behaviour. Another problem with apologising is that when adults apologise to young people it is often followed by the word 'but', in an attempt to legitimise their behaviour, "I'm sorry I shouted at you but you should not have been behaving that way!" Rather than just apologising. We know that one way young people learn to behave is by copying behaviour, so if we want children to apologise appropriately then that's what we should model. It is also important that we teach young people the meaning of the word 'sorry' rather than it just becoming something you say when you have done something wrong.

Body Language

Approximately 7 to 15% of the messages we give are made up of words; the rest of the message comes from the body language, tone and way the message is delivered. Positive body language involves having a relaxed posture and talking with your hands without looking like you are dancing at the Hacienda in the 1980s. An open, sideways stance can help relax people. Our body language can reveal how we are feeling to others for example holding your elbow with one hand whilst the other hand supports your chin could suggest you are anxious about something, whilst standing with your hands on your hips might suggest that you are ready for aggression. In the 1990s doormen used to stand with their arms folded and feet apart directly facing the club goers as they entered the nightclub. This stance almost invited confrontation. Following training, doormen stood sideways and welcomed people in the club. This change in stance not only meant that the clubs were busier because people felt more welcome but also fewer incidents of aggressive behaviour occurred. Body language can be used as a useful behaviour management tool in a classroom, for example, when a class of young people are settled and focused on their task, standing on your toes and scanning the room with a pointed finger can help maintain the positive environment. Simply lifting your chin and looking at all the pupils can also be very powerful. Of course, these techniques may not work for everybody and some staff may feel uncomfortable using them but body language is powerful and should not be underestimated. Research now shows that our body language not only affects how people see us, but it also affects how we see ourselves. If we practice open, confidant body language regularly, evidence shows that we will inevitably become more open and confident. We can use this technique to pretend we are confident, even when we might not be, if we keep on pretending we are confident research shows that we are likely to become confident.

As with all de-escalation techniques, their success depends on the person using them, the person they are being used with and the relationship between these people. Another factor to consider when using de-escalation techniques is where the individual is on the arousal spectrum? The de-escalation techniques above are generally reactive i.e. we react to a certain behaviour with a helpful response.

Post Incident Learning and Support (PILS)

It is extremely important that we learn from mistakes. In his amazing book 'Black Box Thinking' Matthew Syed explores the differences between one of the most dangerous services in the world (The Health Service) and one of the safest services in the world (The Airline Service). Matthew Syed believes that one of the main differences between the two services is that one of the services always learns from mistakes and the other service rarely learns from mistakes. If a pilot makes a mistake they are given a period of anonymity to admit the mistake and often congratulated because the service can now put a system in place to ensure it doesn't happen again, making the airline service, the safest in the world. In comparison in the health service and many other services for that matter, we stigmatized mistakes, we are often punished for mistakes, we see them negatives, this leads to a culture where mistakes are not shared but brushed under the carpet. When mistakes are not shared the only person that can possibly learn something is the person who made the mistake in the first place but sharing the mistake might mean that nobody makes the same mistake again. Young children don't seem to mind making mistakes but as they get older I find they do, I believe that if we want to teach children to behave in a more socially acceptable way, we should not stigmatize the mistakes they make but use them as a learning opportunity.

We sometimes teach behaviour in some very interesting and inventive ways, that we would not consider using to teach children any other subject. Imagine the outcome if a child was publicly moved from a green traffic light to an amber traffic light, or their name was moved from sunshine to cloud, because they got the lowest score in a maths test? Image the outcome if they were made to sit on a 'thinking chair' or shouted at because they made a spelling mistake in a piece of writing. I am sure we would all agree that this approach would be unjustifiable and do little to encourage the child to try harder next time? So why do we sometimes try to teach behaviour in this way, strategies such as the ones above would have a profound, negative impact on a child's maths and spelling skills; such methods could put young people off spellings and maths for the rest of their lives.

During one of my studies, I interviewed 20 young people from a variety of schools and asked them how they thought staff taught them to control their own behaviour. Many young people talked about consequences and punishments for behaviour that included: "making young people stand outside classrooms until the end of the lesson", "getting punished for doing something wrong", "getting shouted at", or "losing golden time". The young people were then asked how they thought these consequences would teach them how to control their behaviour. One pupil responded, "staff think that, if you get punished for doing something wrong, you won't do it again, but we will". Although some of the interviewed young people stated that, if they had "done something wrong", they were told "not to do that again", none of them were aware of any post incident structures for listening and learning; and none of the young people could think of any way that staff taught them how to control their own behaviour. Some young people felt that, "if they needed to speak to someone following an incident, a member of staff would often listen to them" but eighteen out of the twenty young people interviewed explained that, "most staff were not interested", or "did not know how to teach them to control their own behaviour".

In 2005 Infantino and Little examined students' perceptions of classroom behaviour problems and the effectiveness of a variety of disciplinary methods and incentives. The study found that, to improve behaviour, students needed to be educated regarding behavioural expectations.

Logical Consequences

Our priority should be to teach young people how to control their own behaviour, rather than aim to control individuals through fear. So, how do we teach young people to control their own behaviour? Dreikurs and Grey (1993) talked of natural and logical consequences as an effective way of teaching behaviour.

Natural consequences occur as a result of a presented behaviour, for example, if a child refuses to wear gloves in the snow, their hands will become cold; natural consequences such as this, allow young people to experience the unpleasant consequence of their behaviour i.e. cold hands. Of course, there are some natural consequences we need to stop from occurring: if a child is stood in the middle of the road and they are about to get run over, we obviously cannot let this happen, in the hope that the child will learn something. When allowing natural consequences to occur, staff should consider two key factors. Firstly, we need to consider the risk. It is true that we should take calculated risks, but at the same time ensure we are exercising our duty of care and keeping people safe. In the words of the 1989 Children Act, 'The welfare of the child is paramount', but we must consider the risk of not allowing a child to make a mistake. The second factor to consider, when allowing natural consequences to occur, is the desired outcome for the individual. A child with sensory needs may enjoy the feeling of cold hands, so not wearing gloves in the snow may be a way of getting needs met.

Effectiveness of Consequences and punishments

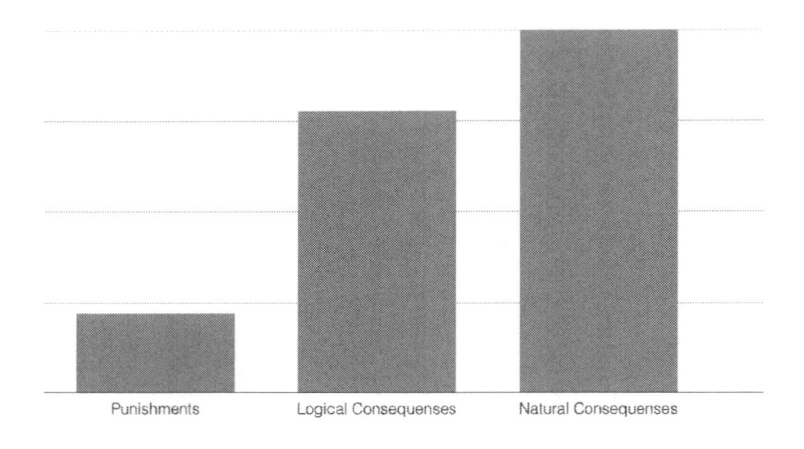

Punishments | Logical Consequenses | Natural Consequenses

The graph above shows the effectiveness of natural consequences, logical consequences and punishments. It has been demonstrated that educating young people through consequences is more effective than the use of punishments (Cotton 2010b). This view was supported by Smith (2005) who studied the impact of detentions where students used the time to complete assignments to improve their academic skills. The study (Smith 2004) concluded that punishment did not improve behaviour, because it did not address the underlying behaviours that warranted the punishment and therefore, completing assignments was not linked to the behaviour exhibited.

Logical consequences are designed by the adult in advance of behaviours, they are logically connected to an exhibited behaviour and should be in proportion to the offence, for example, if a child draws on a table, they could clean the table or, if part of a conflict, the young people involved in the conflict could participate in a conflict resolution process. The key to logical consequences is that if they are to be effective, they should be delivered with support: using the scenario of a child drawing on a desk, asking the child to clean the desk would be a logical consequence; however, if we told the child that they had to clean the desk and they have now lost their playtime, this would be more of a punishment rather than a consequence because the purpose of removing the playtime would be to make the child feel bad about what they had done. Delivering a logical consequence alongside a punishment can severely dilute the effectiveness of the strategy.

A logical consequence involves learning something from the behaviour that has been exhibited, whether it is seen as positive or negative behaviour. When I first discovered the effectiveness of logical consequences, I attempted to write a list of what a logical consequence might be for individual behaviours. It was obvious that asking a pupil to pick up some pens when they have knocked them on to the floor is a logical consequence, but the logical consequence for individuals who have hit someone was not so obvious. Since a logical consequence involves learning something from the exhibited behaviour, talking to an individual following an incident and giving the individual support is in itself a logical consequence for just about every behaviour.

In 1986 Brophy suggested that counselling services, based on the assumption that students lack insight and understanding of their own behaviour, should be a part of an effective discipline programme. Brophy also noted that positive outcomes are reached when students are interviewed and observed, to determine the awareness of their behaviour and the meanings that it holds for them. The study also found that teachers who focus on establishing an effective learning environment need to spend less time responding to behaviour problems and are often more successful than teachers who emphasize their roles as disciplinarians.

One difficulty in providing counselling services for young people could be that of time and training. In 2003 Doyle explained that however sympathetic a person may be, it is unlikely to have a positive impact, if they are not trained in Post Incident Learning structures (PILS). However, highly structured interviews can sometimes be artificial, inflexible and outcomes can be varied Doyle (2003). For this reason, I believe that, due to the logistical problems services might encounter by employing several trained councillors, staff should be trained in very simple structures, based on post incident support methods such as the Life Space Interview (LSI) developed by Redl (1960). The term 'life space' was the area of shared life experience between child and adult and frequently, other children. This was designed by Fritz Redl in 1960 to change a pupil's behaviour patterns by working through a conflict, to help them to recognise the underlying feelings that led to the behaviour. The LSI was designed to help the individual to feel, think and behave in a more socially acceptable way. During the process, the pupil's views would be explored. The member of staff would share their views and connect with other events. The pupil would then be encouraged to consider and plan how the alternative strategies might be put into place, before they, the pupil, were re-entered into their normal routine.

During my time working with young people experiencing social, emotional and behavioural difficulties, I conducted many Life Space Interviews. Although the process did prove to be an effective way of teaching young people how to control their behaviour and led to a reduction in the number of incidents young people were involved in, the process was extremely time consuming, difficult to implement and required in-depth training. (Cotton and Sellman 2004). In 1991 Wood and Long further developed Redl's LSI into the Life Space Crisis intervention (LSCI). The LSCI uses naturally occurring crisis situations as an opportunity to learn, implementing it through a series of six steps:

- Acknowledgment of feelings.
- Discover the pupil's point of view.
- Identify the issue.
- Help recognize and change the behaviour.
- Teach the new skill needed for the change.
- Re-enter the setting.

LSCI is generally considered to be an effective process D'Oosterlinck and Spriet (2006), White-McMahon (2009). In his study examining the effectiveness of LSCI, Ramin (2011) found that positive changes in student behaviours were observed after the introduction of the LSCI. Another study into the effectiveness of LSCI, is that of Dawson (2003) who compared the following student outcomes:

- Frequency of crises,
- Suspension rates,
- Transfers to less restrictive settings,
- Attendance rates

Dawson found that the Life Space Crisis Interview (LSCI) approach in post-incident support was an effective strategy for teaching young people how to control their own behaviour. Following training with staff in two similar schools: 'the experimental school' which received LSCI training and 'the control school' which did not receive the training, but relied on developing their own solutions for crisis. It was found that the frequency of crises and exclusions decreased significantly in the experimental LSCI school. Incidents in the control school increased significantly, young people in the LSCI school also had higher attendance rates. When working with young people experiencing social, emotional and behavioural difficulties, I implemented the LSCI (Wood and Long, 1991) on several occasions, although I found the LSCI process easier to implement, unfortunately no evidence on the effectiveness of LSCI was recorded. In 2010 I explored the basic principles of Redl's 'LSI' and Longs' 'LSCI' and developed them into a Post Incident Learning and Support (PILS) structure.

The key principles of the Post Incident Learning and Support (PILS) structure are:

Listen to the child's point of view first. During this stage the listener should use listening skills such as paraphrasing, summarizing, allowing silence and not making judgments. Although listening suggests auditory *senses,* it is important to understand that we also aim to read the individuals body language and facial expressions.

Link the feeling to the behaviour using questions such as "how did that make you feel?" "so you felt ??????" "and that is why you did that?".

Learn alternative strategies for when the young person feels that way. Staff should explain why they took the action they did. The staff themselves should consider what they could do to support the child better next time. Any consequences should be linked to the behaviour (Dreikurs and Grey 1993). During this stage, it is important that the PILS structure explores the three key areas: the experience, the feelings and the behaviours. This simple approach involves staff in listening to the child's point of view first (Cole, 2009); linking the child's feelings to their behaviour (Faupel, Herrick and Sharp, 1998); and learning alternative behaviours for the next time the child feels that way. This structure can be summarised in three simple questions:

- What happened?
- How did this make you feel?
- What could you do the next time you feel that way?

It is extremely important that these three simple questions form a structure for conversation with the intent of teaching the young person more appropriate behaviours. Timing is crucial and if the young person is still in the depression / recovery phase of the arousal spectrum, peak behaviour may be triggered if individuals push post incident learning. When exploring what happened it is important that staff stay unbiased and avoid making the structure a means of getting to the truth. It can obviously be difficult for adults when they ask "What Happened?" and young person says nothing that resembles the truth, this could be because the young person's perspective on the incident is very different to ours or it might be that the young person is not ready to talk and is still in the recovery / depression phase.

When asking the young people "How did that make you feel?" we could get many responses. Obviously, the best outcome is that the young person explains how they felt. A more common response to this question however is a shrug of the shoulders or "I don't know", these responses highlight a need to develop emotional literacy in our services.

The final question "What could you do the next time you feel that way?" is probably the most important and should not be mistaken with "What can you do the next time that happens?", this is because feelings drive behaviour. If you are feeling tired and something negative happened this might trigger negative feelings which in turn could drive negative behaviour. However, if you were feeling happy and the same negative thing was to happened, the behaviour could be very different.

Cotton (2010b) suggested that using this structure following incidents can improve the outcomes for young people, because it explores the experience, feelings and behaviour of the young people and teaches individuals how to control their own behaviour. The aim of the structure is not only to reduce incidents, but also to improve the outcomes for young people by improving staff/pupil relationships and teaching young people alternative strategies to externalise their feelings.

Communication and Listening

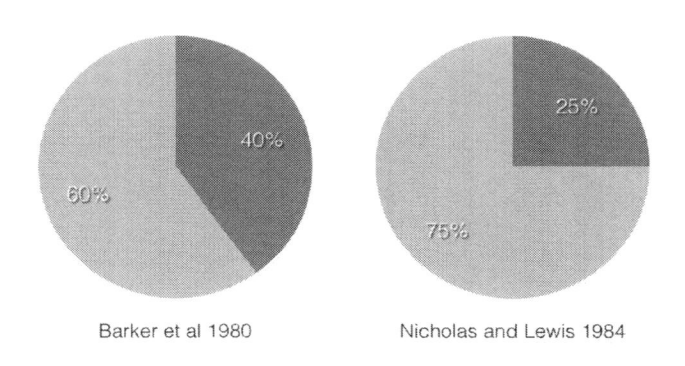

Barker et al 1980   Nicholas and Lewis 1984

Approximately 60% of communication time is spent listening (Barker 1980), but we only retain around 25% of the information we hear (Nicholas and Lewis 1984). If several staff give young people advice, the individual might only take on-board a small amount of the information from each member of staff. This can often lead to confusion and the belief that adults are giving 'mixed messages'. If adults follow a structure, consistency can be improved and the information that is taken on-board is reinforced every time the structure is followed.

"If a drop of water falls on a pebble, eventually it will change the shape of the pebble".

George Matthews 2005

The drop of water would be more efficient at changing the shape of the pebble, if it was continually falling in the same place, highlighting the importance of structure.

During my study (Cotton 2010), two schools catering for young people experiencing social emotional behavioural difficulties (SEBD) were trained in the PILS approach and had implemented it following serious incidents (these were all incidents that involved the use of restrictive physical intervention). Two similar schools catering for young people experiencing SEBD were asked to talk to children following incidents involved physical intervention and give them support, but these two schools were not given any structure to follow. The schools that were trained in PILS, saw a much larger reduction in incidents over a twelve-week period, with one of the schools witnessing a 51% reduction in incidents within 6 months. The two schools that were asked to talk to young people following incidents, but not trained in any structure, saw very little change in the number of incidents, with one school witnessing an increase in such incidents.

Although this was only a small-scale study, it clearly demonstrates that this simple consistent approach to challenging behaviour could be very effective, but when no structure was followed, then the outcomes were varied. If an individual is supported and no structure is followed, outcomes could easily be inconsistent; this could be because, the conversations that take place when no structure is followed, could be influenced by the staff members own experiences, feelings and behaviour.

Although most staff acknowledge the importance of PILS, many staff try to legitimize not using it by statements such as, "We don't have the time". However, Cole (2009) suggests that PILS should not be underestimated and opportunities for such a process should be created; this would require an attitude change within such schools.

During the research (Cotton 2010), it was noted that many staff felt that many young people did not want to talk about incidents. Faupel (1998) suggests that, following a crisis, it can take at least an hour to restore the balance of normal body chemistry; so, young people should be allowed a 'cooling off' period before 'emotional first aid' is attempted. The cooling off time following an incident is dependent on many factors such as the intensity of the incident, the emotional state of the individual etc. Cotton (2010) found that staff might be choosing the wrong time to talk. Insensitive timing was evident in the two schools that did not receive any additional training, but had been asked to try to talk to young people following incidents. In 1998 Faupel *et al*, suggested that training in PILS would support staff in knowing when it is the right 'time' to carry out the process, or when to leave young people to calm. Investing time into PILS reduces incidents, therefore we have more time on our hands, not less.

In 2013, I conducted a further study into the impact of implementing an IT based post-incident learning APP, as an alternative to after school detentions in a mainstream secondary school. When students displayed behaviour, which would normally warrant a detention they were given an APP to complete instead of the detention. It was felt that giving a student a detention alongside the APP would turn the logical consequence of the APP into a punishment and therefore be less effective so the APP was presented and no other consequence or punishment was awarded. Where young people might not want to talk to staff following an incident, or might just give the answers they felt staff wanted to hear; it was thought that an IT based app might be more accessible to young people and this might influence how likely an individual was to carry out Post Incident Learning.

Fig.1

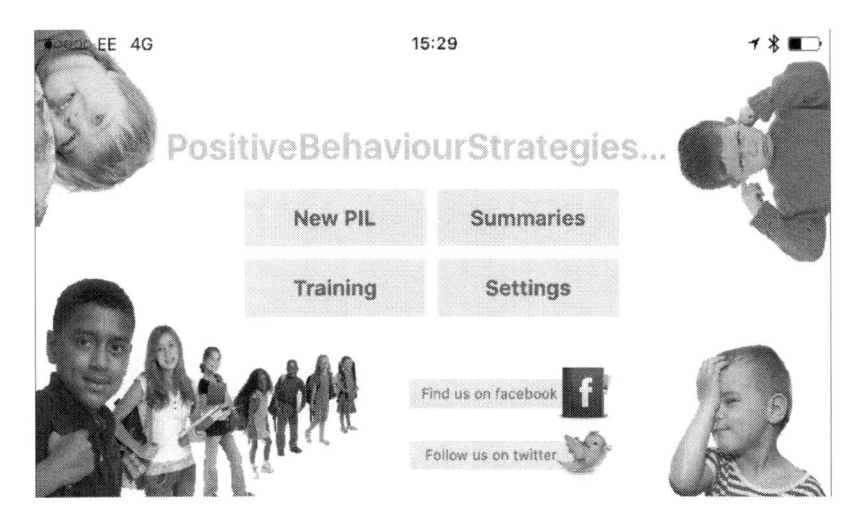

Fig.1 shows the 'Home Page' of the PIL App, on this page the user (Staff or Pupil) can select 'Summaries' to access any previous completed forms, or 'New PIL' to start a new form. The user can also create a password on this page and gain access to previous completed summaries. The App then asks the user the three PILS questions:

- What happened?
- How did this make you feel?
- What could you do the next time you feel that way?

Users can choose to answer by drawing a picture, typing, taking a photograph, or selecting from pre-programmed answers.

NB. 'The Post Incident Learning' APP can be downloaded from Apple App store and Google Play Store.

Although detentions and the belief that such a consequence can support students seems common in secondary education, I believe that addressing the underlying cause of the behaviour is more important, if detentions are going to be reduced and behaviour improved. Additionally, Karande *et al* (2010) suggested that detention could lead to severe emotional stress, loss of self-esteem and further behavioural problems. We know that negative consequences generally drive negative feelings, which in turn can often drive more negative behaviours. This issue is significant when we consider that the Children Act (1989) states that children's welfare should be of paramount importance.

The APP provided consistency and ensured that the PIL structure was always followed. In my study (Cotton 2010b), I noted the importance of structure, but recognised that some students might not want to talk about incidents; the use of the APP made PILS more accessible for these students. I also felt that it was important that the PIL-APP was easy to use and something students could use on their own or with support.

The three questions in the APP are important because my previous studies showed that the most effective PILS structures for behaviour modification, involved exploring experiences (what happened), feelings (how the individual felt when the experience occurred) and behaviour (exploring more socially acceptable behaviours for the next time the individual felt the same), (Cotton 2010a).

For the study, I organised focus group interviews to gather the perceptions of staff and pupils in relation to my research questions. I considered both individual and group interview possibilities and, although aware that group interviews present difficulties, such as the 'risky shift phenomenon' described by Thomas (2009), who recognised that people in groups often make riskier decisions, Hayes (2000) suggested that having focus groups of similar age and sex and ethnicity would go some way towards creating an atmosphere that is permissive and relaxed. I ran four separate focus groups. I believed the benefits of being able to collect a range of voices using a focus group approach, outweighed the disadvantages. Following the introduction of the PIL APP, further quantitative data was collected via the frequency of PIL-APPs awarded to the pupils throughout the intervention.

The focus groups involved in the study included staff from the school, students from the school who had never received detention and students from the school who often receive detention. The results from the focus groups are recorded below.

Focus Group 1 (Ten staff in school)

Focus Group 1 was asked for their views on detentions. One member of staff stated that,

> *"The effectiveness of a detention is determined by how detentions are implemented. If a child is made to sit and do nothing, write lines or the school rules this would have very little impact on the student's behaviour".*

(Focus Group Member, 07.06.2013)

One member of staff gave examples of students not doing homework and being given a detention where they could do their homework under supervision often by a specialist. The member of staff felt that this could improve the effectiveness of detentions and help the student learn.

> *"Detentions should be an education rather than just a sanction"*
> *(Focus Group Member, 07.06.2013)*

Staff believed that detentions were not an effective strategy for repeat offenders, but were effective for students who receive very few detentions for low level incidents, such as being late for class, or handing homework in late.

Staff in this group were shown the APP at the beginning of the focus group meeting. Some staff believed that a post-incident learning structure could be very beneficial and commented that they do this sort of work with young people, but do not follow a specific structure.

Staff in this focus group felt that the PIL-APP would be an effective alternative for detention in schools that did not follow any structure; staff also believed that the PIL-APP could be very useful, if it was readily available and used before a student was awarded a detention. Due to the limited number of devices the school had access to, it was beyond the scope of this study to explore this at this point.

Focus Group 2 (Ten students in school who have never had detention).

This group were shown the PIL-APP at the beginning of the focus group meeting. The group felt that their behaviour in school was down to the way they had been brought up, stating that parents have taught them not to be rude, or 'answer back' to staff. One student stated:

"I am well behaved because I don't want to get a record, which could affect the rest of my life and I don't want people thinking badly of me".
(Focus Group Member, 07.06.2013)

The group believed that they were well behaved because it was the right thing to do, rather than due to the threat of detention.

However, two members of the group felt that the threat of detention was also an important factor.

"You have always got that voice in the back of your head telling you that you could get detention"
(Focus Group Member, 07.06.2013)

The group felt that detentions were ineffective for the students who were constantly awarded them and the PIL-APP was a good alternative to detentions, because it would help teach the students more appropriate ways to deal with feelings. Students felt that the PIL-APP would help students reflect on what they had done wrong and how they could avoid such situations in the future.

"The PIL-APP could be useful if it was used alongside detentions so that students didn't just think that if you were badly behaved it didn't matter because you only had to fill in an APP".
(Focus Group Member, 07.06.2013)

One member of the group felt that, if students had immediate access to the PIL-APP, they could use immediately to avoid getting into trouble and getting detentions. One member of the group felt that the PIL-APP would be useful for lower level behaviours that did not warrant detention. The group raised the concern that, if students did not want to do the PIL-APP, they could just enter irrelevant information to get it completed quickly and then the effectiveness would be questionable. To aid the process, the students felt that having a teacher to support students through the PIL-APP would be beneficial; this view was supported by rotation 3. The group recognized that positive relationships were an important factor in behaviour and, if staff had good relationships with students, the students would respect them and not get detentions.

"If teachers completed the PIL-APP with the student, this could go some way towards building relationships".
(Focus Group Member, 07.06.2013)

The group was asked if their behaviour would be any different if detention was not a consequence that was used in school. The group all agreed that, if detentions were not used in the school, their behaviour would not be any different.

Focus Group 3 (5 staff who used the PIL-APP).

Staff believed that detentions in the school were ineffective and the PIL-APP could be an effective alternative for detentions. One problem staff encountered whilst using the PIL-APP, was that the questions asked were only suitable for behaviours that were driven by feelings and not suitable for a student forgetting their PE kit or being late for school. This had been raised during rotation 2 and was accepted as an issue with the design. Staff reported that when students were asked the question, "what triggered your behaviour?" some students responded with, "what behaviour?"

> *"Some students did not acknowledge that they had done anything wrong"*
> *(Focus Group Member, 07.06.2013)*

It was reported that one student refused to complete the PIL-APP and stated, "it's a waste of time". One member of staff felt that the PIL-APP "worked against them towards the end", because students knew that, irrespective of their behaviour, they could not be punished. This matches the concerns of focus group 2 however; all the staff reported that, although detention was not an option for students, their behaviour did not deteriorate.

> *"PIL-APP had a positive impact on some student behaviour".*
> *(Focus Group Member, 07.06.2013)*

Focus Group 4 (10 students who use the PIL-APP).
Students who used the PIL-APP felt that detentions did not work and were a waste of their time and staff's time.

> *"If detentions worked their behaviour would improve and they would stop getting them, but the fact that we do get detentions, proves that they do not work."*
> *(Focus Group Member, 07.06.2013)*

One student explained that he often gets detention when someone makes him laugh in class. He stated that he has received lots of detentions for this behaviour, but still cannot help laughing when someone makes him laugh.

> *"My parents sometimes get worried when I have detention, especially in the winter when it is dark and I have to go home on the bus."*
>
> *(Focus Group Member, 07.06.2013)*

The students explained that during detentions they are made to copy the school's code of conduct; even though they are made to write this down, they said they did not read what they were writing. The students went on to explain that they knew what was in the code of conduct, but writing it down did nothing to change things.

> *"No punishment would stop me from doing anything, if I wanted to do something, I would".*
>
> *(Focus Group Member, 07.06.2013)*

One student felt that some students fear detentions, so this consequence would work for them, but not for others.

> *"I always get detention for not doing my homework and detention won't make me do my homework, because it's just a minor punishment".*
>
> *(Focus Group Member, 07.06.2013)*

One student explained that, if he gets a detention, he just does not attend and the teacher does not come for him, so the detention is forgotten. Students felt that, a more appropriate response to behaviour, would be for someone to talk to them about what distracts them and teach them ways of not getting distracted.

"If lessons were fun, I wouldn't easily get distracted".
(Focus Group Member, 07.06.2013)

One student found that the PIL-APP was useful, because when he was frustrated, he would normally 'answer back' to teachers, but the PIL-APP taught him stop and count to ten instead; the student explained that, by the time he got to ten, he had usually decided not to answer back.

"The PIL-APP helped me become less distracted in lessons".
(Focus Group Member, 07.06.2013)

Students who used the PIL-APP all found it easier than doing detentions. The group recognised that the PIL-APP proved to be ineffective for late arrival to lessons as this behaviour is generally not driven by a feeling.

Focus group one (Staff in the school) believed that the effectiveness of a detention is determined by how detentions are implemented for example, if a child is made to sit and do nothing, write lines or the school rules, this would have very little impact on the students' behaviour, this view was supported by Van Bockern et al (2008).

Staff in focus group 1 believed that detentions should be an education rather than just a sanction and gave the example of students not doing homework and being given a detention where they can do their homework, under supervision, often by a specialist. Using detentions in this way would be a logical consequence to the behaviour (Dreikurs and Grey 1993). However, this view was contradicted by Conover (1988), who found that detentions for late assignments, did not prove to be an effective deterrent. One student in focus group 4 explained that he often received a detention for not doing his homework and that, during detentions, they are made to copy the schools code of conduct; this contradicted the staff's views on how detentions are used in the school, this indicated an inconsistency in the use of detentions, which could affect the effectiveness of the consequence. Students in this focus group felt that a more appropriate response to behaviour, would be for someone to talk to them about what distracted them and teach them ways of not getting distracted. Following completion of the PIL-APP, staff should talk though the answers that the student inputted.

Staff believed that detentions were not an effective strategy for repeat offenders, but were effective for students who received very few detentions for low level incidents. This view was shared by the students in focus group 2; and, further information from this group suggested, that their 'good' behaviour was more closely linked to, how they had been brought up and that they behaved well, because it was the right thing to do. One member of staff in focus group 3 felt that the PIL-APP "worked against them towards the end", because students knew that, irrespective of their behaviour, they could not be punished; similar views to this were recorded in the focus group 2. However, some of the staff in this focus group explained the PIL-APP had a positive impact on some student behaviour; in addition, behaviour incidents that would normally lead to a detention, were reduced during this research: suggesting that the implementation of PIL-APP did have a positive impact.
With the exception of four students, the sample received fewer PIL-APPs than they had previously received detentions;

therefore, fewer behaviour incidents occurred whilst the PIL-APP was being trialled. No PIL-APPs were awarded to year 11 students from March 2013 to May 2013, so it is unlikely that the reduction in incidents was solely linked to the students' use of the PIL-APP, as they did not experience it. This suggests that something else had an impact on the reduction of incidents. I believe that this is, not just the case in year 11, but it is likely that this is the case throughout the school. If year 11 students had experienced the PIL-APP, we could have been lead to believe that the APP itself was a very effective alternative to detentions.

Improving relationships between staff and students, including a more shared understanding of behaviour expectations and how to manage behaviour incidents, can lead to more positive behaviours. The Post Incident Learning App provided a structure for both staff and students to think about and deal with behaviour incidents. In conclusion, the school saw a 64.5% reduction in behaviour incidents in a three-month period by implementing the Post Incident Learning APP.

Post Incident Learning and Support (PILS) for individuals with communication difficulties.

When I have had a bad day, or I am feeling stressed, I communicate this to my wife and she gives me the support I need (I might just be imagining that). If an individual is unable to communicate how they are feeling, how can they get the support they need?

Mental health conditions in young people are widespread. The number of incidents and the far-ranging implications of such conditions are being reported nationally. Successive governments have approached the support, care and treatment of these conditions in various treatment programmes. Reports published by Action for Happiness (2012) show that there is huge opportunity for improving well-being, with between 21% and 28% of people nationally, reporting low and very low, life happiness. With children and adolescents, we know that this figure is notoriously difficult to predict and to measure (Action for Happiness, 2012), but within this overall category, there is also a sub-set of young people measured on the autistic spectrum, who, for many different reasons, appear to have difficulty accessing therapies.

Although there is no one identifiable cause of mental health problems, some causes may include biological, biochemical, hereditary and psychological factors, although this is part of a much wider debate (MIND, 2012). Following diagnosis, there is a vast array of support therapies available to support people with mental health issues; some of these therapies support the psychological causes of mental health problems (British Association of Behavioural and Cognitive Psychotherapies, 2005).

Although it is recognised that young people are individually resilient, it is fair to assume that, during a stressful incident, most young people will feel anxious or upset. We know that talking to someone about how we feel can often make us feel better and we are then able to continue with everyday life. If we do not talk about how we are feeling and keep things locked inside, feelings often become amplified and, over time this could develop mental health problems.

Autistic spectrum disorder (ASD) is a spectrum of developmental brain disorders, characterized by impaired social interaction and communication skills and a limited range of activities and interests (Kanner 1943). Although autism is not a mental illness (NHS, 2010) over 70% of young people with autism have at least one mental illness / co-morbid disorder (Simonoff, 2008 compared with 9.6% of young people who do not have autism (The Office of National Statistics 2004).

Classical autism, or low functioning autism, is classified by impairment in social interactions and communication. If young people who have classical autism have difficulties in communicating (Kanner, 1943) and, talking therapies involve talking and listening, (DoH, 2001) how can such individuals access these therapies? Improved communication when supporting autistic young people, both pre and post diagnosis, could go some way towards reducing the high co-morbidity rates within this group.

To explore this assertion, I undertook a review of the available and current literature, explored some of the latest available standard talking therapies, that can support an individual with autism following diagnosis of a mental health condition and then, through whole school training sessions, explored how schools proactively support the mental health of their pupils.

Mental health conditions can be supported both proactively and reactively. Proactive mental health support is concerned with how we support individuals prior to and following serious or stressful incidents. Reactive mental health support is concerned with how individuals are supported following the diagnosis of a mental health condition. I explored how a child with autism can access support in both proactive and reactive areas; then developed some observations and techniques that could be employed to improve the way practitioners communicate with low functioning ASD young people.

The National Health Service (NHS) describes autism as a lifelong developmental disability, not a learning disability or mental health problem. The International Classification of Diseases (ICD) categorised autism in ICD-10 as, belonging to the group of "Pervasive Developmental Disorders". Meehan (2011) found three main difficulties in identifying and diagnosing mental health difficulties. These are that people with autism often have difficulties expressing and communicating emotion (Lainhart and Folstein, 1994; Perry, Marston, Hinder, Munden and Roy 2001). There are only limited standardized instruments for the diagnosis of psychiatric disorders in young people with autism (Helverschou, Bakken and Martinsen, 2009); and there is substantial overlap between the behaviours displayed in autism and some symptoms of some mental health problems (Helverschou et al, 2009; Gould, 2010).

In 2004 The Office of National Statistics (ONS) survey found that 9.6% of young people aged between 5 and 16 suffer from a diagnosable mental health disorder, this included 1% of young people with autism. In 2008 Simonoff found that 70% of young people with autism have at least one co-morbid disorder, 41% had two or more.

Meehan, (2011) suggested that although mental health difficulties may have a devastating impact on the lives of those with autism, mental health promotion has been generally overlooked within this group. In 2008, Jones, English, Guldberg, Jordan, Richardson and Waltz found that many autistic young people are managed in primary schools, but often find secondary schools very difficult and can develop significant mental health and behavioural difficulties.

Madders (2010) described autism as a complex disability, making co-morbid mental health problems harder to recognize, harder to evaluate and harder to treat. Atkinson and Hornby (2002), Music (2007) and Tyler (2010) found that staff in schools often felt that supporting young people's mental health was outside their remit. Other reports suggest a lack of teacher knowledge in this area

(Atkinson and Hornby, 2002; Weare and Gray, 2003; Department of Health, 2006. Other barriers against supporting mental health issues in schools include, the role of the National Curriculum (O'Hanlon, 2000) and testing and league tables (Finney, 2006).

There are many conventional approaches to treating mental health problems, with an important set being talking therapies. Talking therapies cover a range of interventions that help people deal with negative feelings (The Mental Health Foundation, 2012). The MHF also believe that talking about your problems is an important factor for good mental health. The National Institute for Health and Clinical Excellence (NICE) in 2005 recommended talking therapies, rather than medicine, for young people who have depression. NICE guidelines state that good communication between healthcare professionals and young people is essential and, that the support provided, should be tailored to the needs of the individual and that the physician should be fully informed of the preferred communication style of the individual (Howlin, 1997).

Structured post incident learning is a technique for learning through reflection, sharing experiences, gathering information and developing ideas for the future (Gibbs, 1988). My study into the effect that structured post incident learning has on pupils and schools, following serious incidents (Cotton, 2010), found that a structured process for post incident learning reduces incidents by teaching young people more socially acceptable ways of expressing their need for support thus improving the mental health of the child (MHF, 2012). However, lack of structure could make post incident learning less effective (Kahan, 1994).

Although structured post incident support may be difficult for young people with classical autism, individuals have a human right to be listened to (Taylor, 2000). The Disability Discrimination Act and the Equality Act (2010) make it a legal requirement for reasonable adjustments to be made to the services provided to people with disabilities, including autism. As well as there being a legal responsibility and duty to do something, we need to find some solutions to this problem.

The National Autistic Society (2012) stated that communication and interaction do not have to involve the use of language and speech, so other methods of communication need to be established. We know that there are many traditional speech and language tools and communication aids in existence, such as the Picture Exchange Communication System (PECS) and that these can be useful in the delivery of talking therapies, such as Cognitive Behaviour Therapy (CBT). What is less clear, is whether or not, these tools are used by therapists and practitioners with young people with autism and how effective they are in helping young people gain access to therapy. PECS was developed by Bondy and Frost (1994) and is designed to address the needs of young people with significant communication deficits. Bondy and Frost's study (1994) showed that 95% of 85 non-verbal pre-school children with autism had learned to use the picture symbols for communicating. Other communication aids that could be used to support the delivery of talking therapies might include, Alternative and Augmentative Communication (AAC) systems. These systems support or replace spoken communication. The techniques include gesture, symbols, signing, word boards, communication boards, books and Voice Output Communication Aids (VOCAs) (Scope, 2012). Voice Output Communication Aids (VOCAs) are a commercially available electronic device designed to support people who are unable to vocalize their needs and exchange information. Communication passports (Miller, 1997) can also be used to support the delivery of talking therapies.

Communication passports are a positive way of supporting people with sensory and communication disabilities who cannot speak for themselves. The communication passport includes personal information about the child's needs, such as his/her likes and dislikes. The passport is owned by the child and helps new people understand a child's personal needs (Scope, 2012). Although Goldbart and Caton (2010) could find no formal evaluation of communication passports, 30% of practitioners involved in the research, reported using communication passports. The research of (Goldbart and Caton, 2010) found that the passports were used more with adults than young people. There are many therapeutic approaches for supporting mental health, many of which feature long-term interventions such as counselling. There appears to be some welcome signs that the needs of particularly high functioning autistic young people can be met through counselling. Counselling covers a broad spectrum of interventions, but provides a regular time and space for people to talk about their troubles. This is done in an environment that is free from intrusion and is confidential, so people are encouraged to explore difficult feelings (MIND, 2012).

In 2006, Vermeulen and Vanspranghe found that counselling can help to resolve misinterpretations of the world, held by those with autism, which can lead to anxiety however, The National Institute of Deafness and other Communication Disorders (NIDCD) recognise that young people with classical autism are often self-absorbed and seem to exist in a private world, where they are unable to successfully communicate and interact, making the counselling process difficult with this group. Other forms of counselling include the Life Space Interview (LSI) and the Life Space Crisis Intervention (LSCI).

Cognitive Behaviour Therapy (CBT) is a talking therapy that was popularized by Burns (2008). It is based on the principle that certain ways of thinking can trigger mental health problems. CBT can help clients to analyse existing thinking patterns, emotional reactions and behaviour, which are identified via an 'assessment of difficulties'. CBT encourages clients to try new approaches to thoughts and feelings.

A growing body of research has supported the value of CBT. Elliot and Place (1998) stress that CBT is an effective way of altering peoples thinking patterns for the better. Other research (Stallard 2009) suggests that, if CBT is delivered via a celebrative partnership and individuals are committed and persistent in tackling and improving their problem, CBT can have long-term benefits and teach individuals involved techniques that can be used for a lifetime. However, Willson and Branch stress that CBT does not suit everyone and it is not helpful for all conditions. Lynch et al found that CBT is of no value in schizophrenia and has limited effect on depression.

The Royal College of Psychiatrists (2012) found that Cognitive Behaviour Therapy (CBT) is particularly appropriate for people with autism or Asperger's syndrome, as it can be used to challenge cognitive distortions (Paxton and Estay, 2007). CBT is a way of talking about how you think about yourself, the world and other people and how your actions affect other people.

The concept of CBT was developed by Pavlov in 1897. This stemmed from applying the principles of learning theory to shape human behaviour, and this in turn, through altering behaviour may help to alleviate psychological disorders. Two examples of Computerised CBT have been approved by the National Health Service (NHS). Evidence suggests that the delivery of CBT using a computer can help with anxiety and depressive disorders especially when a patient also sees a therapist (NHS, 2010).
Wood, Drahota, Sze, Har, Chiu and Langer (2009) randomly assigned 40 young people with autism, ranging from seven to eleven years old, to 16 sessions of CBT or a three-month waiting

list for CBT. Parents and young people completed anxiety symptom checklists at the point of baseline and post treatment / post waiting list. The research found that 78.5% of the CBT group met Clinical Global Impressions (CGI) scale criteria, compared with only 8.7% of the waiting list group. The CGI scale is one of the most widely used assessment instruments in psychiatry, the scale offers a readily understood, practical tool that can be easily used by clinicians (Busner and Targum, 2007). The research found that remission of anxiety disorders appeared to be an achievable goal among high-functioning young people with autism. Ooi, Lam, Sung, Tan, Goh, Fung, Pathy, Ang and Chua (2008) also found that 16 sessions of CBT was effective in reducing anxiety in high functioning autistic young people with a mean age of 11.50 years.

Sofronoff, Attwood and Hinton (2005) also evaluated young people diagnosed with Asperger's Syndrome who received CBT and the impact of parental involvement. Parent involvement enhanced the usefulness of the intervention.

Most academics and clinicians consider CBT to be an effective therapy for some individuals, but it is not without its limitations,

"1. The precise role of cognitive processes is yet to be determined. The maladaptive cognitions seen in psychologically disturbed people could be a consequence rather than a cause.

2. The cognitive model is narrow in scope - thinking is just one part of human functioning, broader issues need to be addressed.

3. Ethical issues: CBT is a directive therapy aimed at changing cognitions sometimes quite forcefully. For some, this may be considered an unethical approach."
(McLeod 2008).

Whilst studying CBT I contacted fifteen CBT Practitioners randomly selected from the British Association for Behavioural & Cognitive Psychotherapies (BABC) website. The website lists the contact details and specialisms of practitioners who are registered with the organisation. The fifteen practitioners I contacted all specialised in working with young people with autism. The specialists were asked how young people with classical autism were supported through CBT?

Twelve out of the fifteen practitioners stated that, they only worked with autistic young people, if the individuals had some level of language. Fourteen of the practitioners stated that, they found the process of CBT difficult with this group, due to the perceived level of communication such young people display (Hall, 1996). The three practitioners, who worked with young people who have classic autism, explained that they often needed to be more creative in their approach, but did not explain how they were creative and what this involved.

The research seemed to suggest that although CBT is or can be extremely effective, access for the individuals who need it most can be extremely limited.

In 2012 I produced a paper, which explored the communication strategies that can be used to support the mental health of young people with classical autism. For this study, two schools offering education for young people with a wide range of special educational needs, including young people with autistic spectrum disorder (ASD), profound and multiple learning disabilities (PMLD), severe learning disabilities (SLD) and complex medical conditions, were approached and asked to be take part in this study. The whole staff team in each school was trained in providing structured post incident support for young people with ASD, in order to proactively support the young people's mental health. With support, the two schools then developed a range of PILS strategies. The strategies were then trialled with young people for one term and the views of the staff were then recorded, via whole school staff meetings. The age and performance levels (P-Levels), (Qualifications and Curriculum Authority, 2005) of the young people involved in the study, were collected to give an idea of each child's level of communication. The young people in the study were aged between 11 and 15 with P-Levels in Speaking / Expressive communication between 4 and 6 (see appendix 2 for explanation of P-Levels)

All the staff in the schools understood the importance of building positive relationships with the young people that they support and understood that the key to building positive relationships was to share positive experiences with the young people. Building positive relationships, enables staff to spot signs of anxiety and intervene early. The use of communication passports enabled staff to react to each child's needs in a personalised way. These were completed with the young people and shared among the staff team, parents and other professionals. One school used a communication dictionary to record how young people communicate and ways in which staff can help young people to feel better.

The following worksheets were used following incidents where a child had become upset. The worksheets were completed by staff and young people and used as evidence of how staff had tried to rebuild a positive relationship after an incident. Either the pupil or the staff member could draw what happened during the incident. The worksheet was laminated, so that, when the pupil had given as much information as s/he feels s/he could manage, it could be photocopied and the pupil wiped the worksheet clean.

Me	This Happened?	I felt?

If I feel like this again I will….

Pupil…………..
Staff ………….
Date …………..

The smiley and sad faces (below) were used in one of the schools to teach young people basic feelings such as happy and sad. The teacher would show pupils the different faces, depending on the situation, for example, if a child did a good piece of work or was particularly helpful, the child would be shown the happy face. If a child showed unacceptable behaviour e.g. violence towards another child, the child was shown the unhappy face. Staff tried to ensure that the happy face was shown more that the unhappy face.

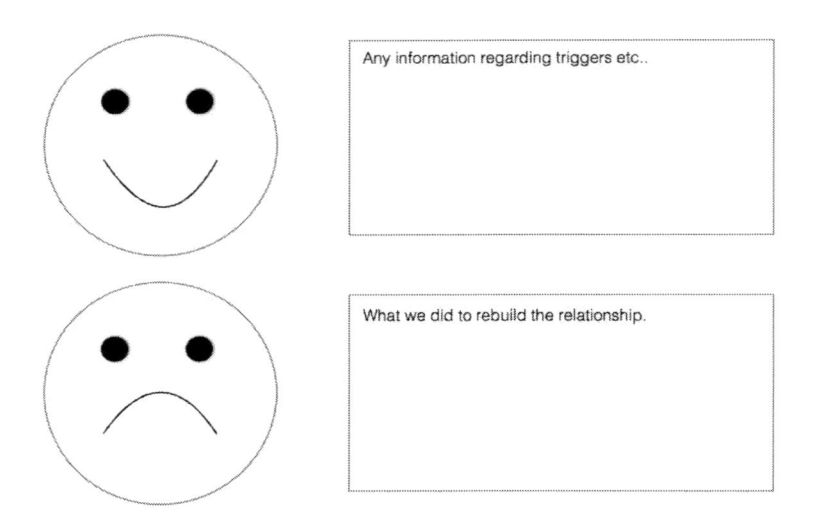

☺	Any information regarding triggers etc..
☹	What we did to rebuild the relationship.

The Picture Exchange Communication System (PECS) Symbols were also used by one of the schools to teach young people about different feelings. In another of the schools involved, PECS symbols accompanied stories and were also used for post incident support. Some young people found the coloured symbols over stimulating, so the colour was removed for such young people.

One of the schools developed 'feelings diaries' (a sample of which can be found below). The diary was completed by young people and staff at the end of each day and would go some way towards helping staff recognise how individuals were feeling. The feelings in the feelings diary were selected upon completion of the emotional assessment tool earlier in this book.

My Feelings Diary

Happy   Sad

Day 1

Things that made me feel happy today.

Things that made me feel sad happy today.

Day 1

Overall today I felt

☺
☐
Because…

☹
☐
Because

The experiences, feeling, behaviour worksheet below was completed with a child, post incident and then wiped clean by the child.

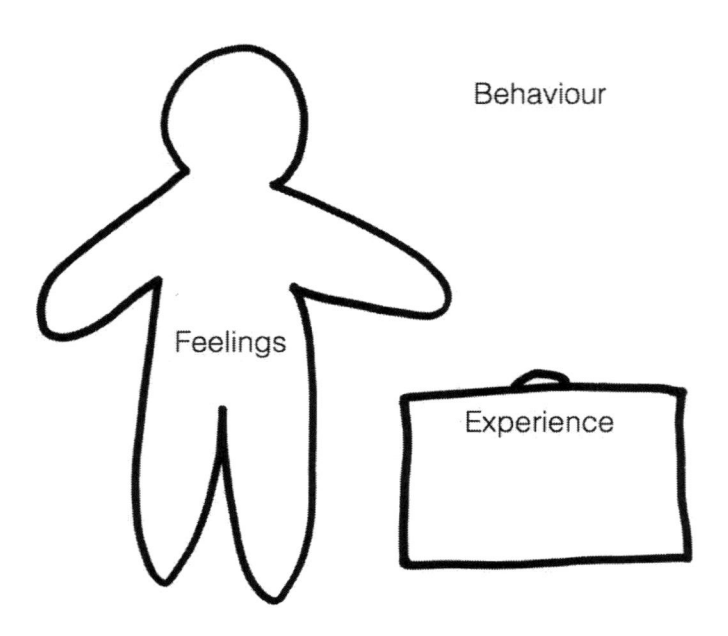

The listen, link, learn, worksheet is another example of the experiences, feelings, behaviour worksheet.

Listen (What happened?)

Link (How did it make you feel?)

Learn (What could you do if you feel that way again?)

One of the schools involved in the research felt that the strategies they implemented went some way towards enabling the staff to build positive relationships with the young people they work with. The school believed that the consistent implementation of the strategies would support the mental health of their young people in the long term. The staff stated that they would continue to implement the strategies and reassess the long-term impact in the future. The Head of this school stated that implementing these strategies had a positive impact on the ethos of the school.

Mental health conditions in young people are widespread (Action for Happiness, 2012 and ONS, 2004) and although there is no one identifiable cause of mental health problems, it is generally accepted that talking about problems can go some way to ensuring improved and hopefully, more manageable mental health (MHF, 2012). Young people with classical autism often have difficulties in communicating their problems and research suggests that 70% of autistic young people exhibit one or more co-morbid disorder (ONS, 2004).

One reason for such high rates of co-morbidity within this group could be due to the difficulties autistic young people have in communicating. If a child is unable to communicate how they are feeling, how can they get the support they need? Personal Communication Plans (PCP's) could be used so that parents, teachers and other professionals know the child's individual style of communication, enabling more effective support for the child.

The two schools involved in the research managed to implement several strategies aimed at improving communication with young people with classical autism. Although the impact of the implementation of the strategies is difficult to assess, both schools reported positive outcomes through implementing the strategies such as enabling the staff to build more positive relationships with the young people. Completing the work sheet with the child could go some way towards building relationships especially if the worksheet was shared on completion. The staff in the school, which took part in this study, all recognised that building positive relationships with the young people would enable them to spot early signs of anxiety and intervene appropriately. One school also commented on an improved ethos within the school as a direct result of the implementation of the strategies. This could be because the strategies encouraged the staff and young people to share positive experiences.

A major obstacle to supporting mental health could be that autism is a complex disability. The limited standardized instruments for diagnosis (Perry, 1994), also make mental health problems difficult to assess (Action for Happiness, 2012). However, Atkinson et al, (2002) explained that the everyday pressure of work for teachers, combined with a lack of teacher knowledge and teachers often feeling that mental health promotion is outside their remit, is also a major disadvantage in supporting the mental health of the young people with autism. This could be one reason why mental health promotion has been generally overlooked within this group (Meehan, 2011) but research shows that, if these obstacles could be overcome, the mental health of the autistic child could be supported (MHF, 2012).

More support for teachers, plus quality training in recognising and supporting mental health issues in young people, along with the development of more instruments for diagnosis, could go some way towards reducing the high rates of co-morbidity in this group. There are many communication aids that are available to support communication these methods could be used to support the mental health of the autistic child, both pre and post diagnosis. Following diagnosis of a mental health condition, CBT and other talking therapies, could go some way towards reducing co-morbidity in autistic young people (Ooi et al 2008). CBT was highlighted by Paxton and Estay, (2007) as particularly appropriate for people with autism.

The evidence, whilst far from clear, appears to suggest that on the one hand young people with autism appear to benefit, as do most young people, from therapy (MHF, 2012). Yet on the other hand, there remains the questions about access and relevance, in terms of choosing the right therapy in a crowded field and arguably, questions of validity and evaluated impact. My initial research backed up the assertion that there is variable practice, different approaches, a lack of consistency, perhaps in application and consequently, variable outcomes. Yet, what seems to link practitioners approaches together, is a recognition that in fact young people with autism seem to struggle to gain access to these services.

Mental Health could be supported in education, because the simple strategies developed and implemented by the two schools, had positive outcomes and could in turn, support a young person's mental health, proactively.

If post incident learning and support is an effective strategy to teach people more socially acceptable behaviour and support the mental health of the individual, it is important that we consider ways of implementing the process with young people with a variety of needs. It might not always be possible to achieve this; there are people that might not be able to access the process, but this does not mean that the process cannot be implemented.

Based on the idea that young people need certain skills to benefit from PILS it might be that we need to work on the skills required whist carrying out PILS. The two main skills required are listening skills and a level of emotional literacy. Below is a non-exhaustive list of tools we can use to develop listening skills:

- Use of Body language
- Facial expression
- Eye pointing
- Objects of reference
- Communication aids
- Augmentative/alternative communication
- Routine
- Information Technology
- Use of Intonation
- Photos, pictures, symbols
- Print
- Signing
- Sounds / spoken word
- Facilitated communication
- Social interaction
- Intensive interaction
- Sound walks
- Sound game

Below in a non-exhaustive list of tools that can be used to develop emotional intelligence:

- Emotion Jigsaws
- Feelings Diaries
- Emotion Pictures
- Social Stories
- Art
- Drama
- iPad Apps such as Post Incident Learning
- Feelings of the week
- Emotion Displays
- Feelings Stories
- Films
- Sharing feelings

Focusing on the development of listening skills and emotional intelligence help young people take positive steps towards learning from incidents and getting support.

Sometimes we need to think outside the box and if we understand what we are trying to achieve, this can make things easier. We want the individual to feel supported. This might take the form of giving the young person a hug, or talking to them in a soft, supportive voice. We also want the individual to learn from their actions. This might take the form of implementing a logical consequence or allowing a natural consequence to take place, without putting the individual in danger.

Sometimes we do not know how much information an individual with autism is taking on-board, but people have surprised us with their level of understanding on many occasions. A 12 year old boy with nonverbal autism learned to express himself through Rapid Processing Method (RPM) and showed himself to be an amazing writer: cases like this are not uncommon.

One of the most common problems in care and education settings in relation to post incident learning and support is that of time. Not only does the use of PILS reduce incidents therefore giving us more time to do other things but PILS has many other benefits.

Support Mental Health.

We know that talking about problems can help us build relationships and good quality relationships have a positive effect on our mental health. PILS enables people to check the welfare of individuals and shows that we care about them.

Improved Emotional Intelligence.

It is not always easy to talk about feelings and some people find it difficult to describe feelings. We often feel more than one feeling simultaneously which makes linking feelings to names of feelings even more difficult. Using PILS regularly encourages discussions around feelings and has been show to improved emotional intelligence which can lead to improved communication and ultimately improved behaviour.

Explore triggers.

PILS can help us identify triggers to behaviour so that we can best support the individual when they are exposed to the trigger. As discussed earlier, it is a common misconception in some services that we should avoid triggers but through PILS we teach strategies to deal with triggers rather than just avoiding them giving individuals lifelong skills.

Facilitate Learning.

Because we learn more from mistakes than we do successes we can use PILS to facilitate learning, reducing incidents and improving behaviour. We can also use PILS to learn from each other developing a greater understanding of individual needs. The key to PILS is that everyone has an entitlement to it and communication is not a young person's problem, it is a problem for those staff who are supporting the individual. If I told you *in English* that I was feeling stressed, you would probably be able to support me, but if I told you I was stressed in Chamicuro (a language that is only spoken by 8 people who mainly live in Peru), you might have a problem, but it's your problem not mine.

> *Everybody is a Genius. But If You Judge a Fish by Its Ability to Climb a Tree, It Will Live Its Whole Life Believing that It is Stupid*
>
> *Albert Einstein*

Appendix 1

My Plan

Name: Date of Plan: Review Date of Plan:

What does my behaviour look like?

Stage 1 Trigger Behaviours	Stage 2 Escalation Behaviours	Stage 3 Peak Behaviours
My Behaviour:	My Behaviour:	My Behaviour:
What I can do to help myself?	What I can do to help myself?	What I can do to help myself?
What can adults do to help?	What can adults do to help?	What can adults do to help?
Stage 4 Depression	Stage 5 Recovery	Stage 6 Follow up
My Behaviour:	My Behaviour:	My Behaviour:
What I can do to help myself?	What I can do to help myself?	What I can do to help myself?
What can adults do to help?	What can adults do to help?	What can adults do to help?

What are my triggers?

What do I like?

1.
2.
3.
4.
5.

De-escalation skills

	Try	Avoid	Notes
Verbal advice and support	☐	☐	_____
Giving space	☐	☐	_____
Reassurance	☐	☐	_____
Help scripts	☐	☐	_____
Negotiation	☐	☐	_____
Limited Choices	☐	☐	_____
Humour	☐	☐	_____
Logical Consequences	☐	☐	_____
Tactical ignoring	☐	☐	_____
Take up time	☐	☐	_____
Time-out	☐	☐	_____
Supportive touch	☐	☐	_____
Transfer adult	☐	☐	_____
Success reminded	☐	☐	_____
Simple listening	☐	☐	_____
Acknowledgement	☐	☐	_____
Apologising	☐	☐	_____
Agreeing	☐	☐	_____
Removing audience	☐	☐	_____
Others	☐	☐	_____

Are there any factors to consider when debriefing? For example, Communication aids, staff etc.

Listen **Link** **Learn**	

Parents/Carers: Name:
Teacher   Name:
Social services (if applicable)   Name:
Educational Psychologist   Name:
Case Worker   Name:
Young Person   Name:

Appendix 2

P-Level 4

"Pupils repeat, copy and imitate between 10 and 50 single words, signs or phrases, or use a repertoire of objects of reference or symbols. They use single words, signs and symbols for familiar objects, for example, 'cup', 'biscuit', and to communicate about events and feelings, for example, likes and dislikes".

P-Level 6

P6 Pupils initiate and maintain short conversations using their preferred medium of communication. They ask simple questions to obtain information, for example, 'Where's cat?'. They can use prepositions, such as 'in' or 'on', and pronouns, such as 'my' or 'it', correctly.

In Listening / Receptive communication the pupils in the study had P-level between 4 and 7.

P-Level 4

P4 Pupils demonstrate an understanding of at least 50 words, including the names of familiar objects. Pupils respond appropriately to simple requests that contain one key word, sign or symbol in familiar situations, for example, 'Get your coat', 'Stand up' or 'Clap your hands'.

P-Level 7

P7 Pupils listen to, attend to and follow stories for short stretches of time. They follow requests and instructions with four key words, signs or symbols, for example, 'Get the big book about dinosaurs from the library'. They attend to, and respond to, questions from adults and their peers about experiences, events and stories, for example, 'Where has the boy gone?'.

Qualifications and Curriculum Authority, 2005

REFERENCES

Allen, B. & Matthews, G. (2003) Team-Teach Work Book. St. Leonards on Sea: Steaming Publications.

Action for Happiness, 2012. http://www.actionforhappiness.org/news/first-world-happiness-report-launched-at-united-nations 15.8.12.

Association for Cognitive Analytical Therapy, 2012. Association for Cognitive Analytical Therapy. http://www.acat.me.uk/page/about+cat 18.6.12

Atkinson, M and Hornby, G. 2002. Mental Health Handbook for Schools. London: Routledge.

Autism Network. (2010). Picture Exchange Communication System Introduction. Available: http://www.autismnetwork.org/modules/comm/pecs/index.html. Last accessed 26 May 2010

Bandura, A. (1965). Influence of models' reinforcement contingencies on the acquisition of imitative responses. Journal of personality and social psychology, 1(6), 589.

Bell, J. 2005. Doing your Research Project: A guide for first-time researchers in education, health and social science. Maidenhead. Open University Press

Bondy, A and Frost L, 1994. The Picture Exchange Communication System. Focus on Autism and Other Developmental Disabilities, Vol. 9, No. 3, 1-19

British Association for Behavioural and Cognitive Psychotherapies (BABCP) Mapping Psychotherapy, 2005. What is CBT? http://www.babcp.com/silo/files/what-is-cbt.pdf

British Educational Research Association (2011). Ethical Guidelines for Educational Research. London: BERA

Brophy, J. (1986). Classroom Management Techniques. Education and urban society, 18(2), 182-94.
Busner ,J and Targum,S, 2007. The Clinical Global Impressions Scale, Applying a Research Tool in Clinical Practice, Psychiatry (Edgmont) 2007 July; 4(7): 28-37

Centre for Economic Performance, 2012. How mental illness loses out in the NHS. London: The London School of Economics and Political Science

Cohen, L., Manion, L., & Morrison, K. (2004). A guide to teaching practice. Psychology Press.

Cole, R. Purao, S. Rossi, M. and Sein, M.K (2005). Being Proactive: Where Action Research Meets Design Research. Proceedings of the Twenty- Sixth International Conference on Information Systems, Las Vegas, pp. 325-336.

Cole, T.(2009). Positive Behaviour Management: characteristics of effective mainstream schools. Study and Information Pack B (09/10). Curriculum and Caring for Children with SEBD: Theory and Practice. Manchester, SEBDA

Cole T, Daniels H & Visser J (2002) the health needs of young people with emotional and behavioural difficulties – bright futures: working with vulnerable young people

Conover P,J. (1988) Detention as a deterrent for late assignments: A study. Paper presented at the annual meeting of the American Research Association. Boston, MA. (ERIC Document Reproduction Service N: ED325910)

Cotton, D. (2010a). Effectiveness of Team-Teach. Manchester: SEBDA

Cotton, D, (2010b). The effect structured listening and learning has on pupils and schools following incidents involving physical intervention. http://www.pbstraining.co.uk/category/members/ Last accessed 15.8.13

Cotton, D. and Sellman, E. (2004). SEBDA News, Achieving Gold: 'Team-Teach' Behaviour Management Approach. SEBDA : Manchester.

Cotton, K. and Savard, WG. (1982). Student Discipline and Motivation: Research Synthesis. NW Regional Educational Laboratory. Portland: Oregon.

Dawson, C. (2003). A study on the effectiveness of life space crisis intervention for students identified with emotional disturbances. Reclaiming Children and Youth. Michigan: Gale Group.

Department for Children, Schools and Families. (2010). School discipline and pupil behaviour policies, guidance for schools. London: DCSF

Department for Education, (2012). Behaviour and discipline in schools, A guide for head teachers and school staff. London: DfE.

Department for Education, (2013). Use of reasonable force A guide for head teachers, staff and governing bodies. London: DfE.

Department for Education and Skills (DfES) and the Department of Health (DOH) (2002) The guidance for restrictive physical interventions. London;
Department for Education and Skills and the Department of Health

Department of Health, 2001. Choosing Talking Therapies. London: Department of Health.

Department of Health, 2006. Promoting the mental health and psychological well-being of children and young people: report on the implementation of Standard 9 of the National Service Framework for Children, Young People and Maternity Services. London: Department of Health.

DeMagistris, R. & Imber, S.C. (1980). The effects of the life space interview on academic and social performance of behaviourally disordered secondary students. Behavioural Disorders, 6(1); 12-25

DfES, (2005). Social and Emotional Aspects of Learning (SEAL): Improving behaviour, improving learning :DfES 2005

Doyle, CE. (2003). Work and Organizational Psychology: An Introduction with Attitude. East Sussex: Psychology Press

Dreikurs, R. and Grey, L. (1993). The New Approach to Discipline, Logical Consequences. New York: Plume.

Education Act 1996. (c.550b). London: HMSO.

Elliott, J. (1991). Action Research for Educational Change. Milton Keynes: Open University Press.

Ellison, S (2002) Taking the War Out of Our Words: The Art of Powerful Non-Defensive Communication: Bay Tree Publishing

Faupel, A Herrick, E and Sharp, P, 1998. Anger Management A Practical Guide. London. David Fulton Publishers

Finney, D. 2006. Stretching the boundaries: schools as therapeutic agents in mental health. Is it a realistic proposition? Pastoral Care, September 2006, 22-27

Freud, A. 1937. The Ego and the Mechanisms of Defence. London: Hogarth Press and Institute of Psycho-Analysis.

Gibbs, G. 1988 Learning by Doing: A guide to teaching and learning methods. Further Education Unit. Oxford Polytechnic: Oxford.

Goldbart, J Caton, S. 2010. Communication and people with the most complex needs: What works and why this is essential. Research Institute for Health and Social Care. Manchester Metropolitan University (MMU) : Manchester.

Gould, J. 2010. Autism Spectrum Disorders and Mental Health and Implications for Diagnosis and Support. Presentation at Autism Special Interest Group for Educational Psychologists. London, 12.7.10.

Gray, C. 1991. What Are Social StoriesTM. Available: http://www.thegraycenter.org/social-stories/what-are-social-stories. Last accessed 7.6.12

Hall, L. 1996 The generalization of social skills by preferred peers with autism. Journal of Intellectual & Developmental Disability, 21(4), pp313-131.

Hayes, N. (2000). Doing Psychological Research: A Guide to Practice. Buckingham: Open University Press

Helverschou, S.B., Bakken, T.L. and Martinsen, H. 2009. The psychopathology in autism checklist (PAC): A pilot study. Research in Autism Spectrum Disorders, 3, (1). 170-195

Heneker S (2005) Speech and language therapy support for pupils with behavioural, emotional and social difficulties (BESD) a pilot project. British Journal of Special Education Vol 32 no 2

Howlin, P. 1997. Autism: Preparing for Adulthood. London: Routledge.

HMSO (1989). Children's Act, London: Her Majesty's Stationery Office.

Infantino, J. and Little, E. (2005).Students' Perceptions of Classroom Behaviour Problems and the Effectiveness of Different Disciplinary Methods: Educational Psychology 25(5)491–508

Johnson, L. (2004). The Queen of Education. San Francisco: Jossey-Bass.

Jones, G, English, A, Guldberg, K, Jordan, R. Richardson, R. and Waltz, M. 2008 Educational provision for children and young people on the autism spectrum living in England: a review of current practice, issues and challenges. London: Autism Education Trust.

Kahan, B. 1994 Growing up in Groups. London: HMSO

Kanner, L. 1943 Disturbances of Affective Contact. Nervous Child 2, 217-250

Karande, S., & Gogtay, N. J. (2010). Specific learning disability and the right to education 2009 act: Call for action. Journal of Postgraduate Medicine, 56(3), 171.

Lainhart, J.E. and Folstein, S.E. 1994 Affective disorders in people with autism: a review of published cases. Journal of Autism and Developmental Disorders, 24, (5), 587-601

Lefton, L. A. (1991). Psychology. Boston: Allyn and Bacon.

Long, N. and Morse, W. (1996). Conflict in the Classroom: The Education of At-Risk and Troubled Students. Austin: Pro-Ed.

Long, N. J., Wood, M. M., & Fecser, F. A. (2001). Life space crisis intervention: Talking with children and youth to improve relationship and change behaviours. Austin, TX: PRO-ED, Inc

Madders, T. 2010. You Need to Know. Campaign Report. London: National Autistic Society.

Martin, R. (2013) Aston academics research effectiveness of speed awareness courseshttp://www.aston.ac.uk/about/news/releases/2013/january/speed-awareness-courses/ Last accessed September 2015

McLeod, S. A. 2008. Cognitive Behavioural Therapy. http://www.simplypsychology.org/cognitive-therapy.html 4.7.12

Meehan, L 2011 The mental health of young people with autism and Asperger syndrome in mainstream secondary schools: a multiple case study approach. Birmingham : University of Birmingham

Mental Health Foundation, 2012. http://www.mentalhealth.org.uk/help-information/10-ways-to-look-after-your-mental-health/ 31.5.12

Mental Health Foundation, 2012. Talking Therapies. Available: http://www.mentalhealth.org.uk/help-information/mental-health-a-z/T/talking-therapies/. Last accessed 30.5.12

Miller, S. 1997 Personal Communication Passports Information Pack (5), CALL Centre, University of Edinburgh

MIND, 2012. MIND http://www.mind.org.uk/help/medical_and_alternative_care/making_sense_of_counselling#whatis 18.6.12

Moffat, B (2010) Debriefing structure for pupils with limited communication (Unpublished)

National Autistic Society, 2012 http://www.autism.org.uk/living-with-autism/communicating-and-interacting/communication-and-interaction.aspx 25.7.12

National Health Service, 2012. http://www.nhs.uk/Livewell/Autism/Pages/Autismoverview.aspx 23.8.12

National Health Service, 2010. NHS http://www.nhs.uk/Conditions/Cognitive-behavioural-therapy/Pages/How-does-it-work.aspx 18.6.12

National institute on Deafness and other communication disorders NIDCD, 2012.

National institute of Health, 2012. http://www.nidcd.nih.gov/health/voice/pages/autism.aspx 20.6.12

NICE, 2005. Latest NICE guidance sets new standards for treating depression in children and young people: NHS 2005

Office for Standards in Education, 2009. The exclusion from school of children aged four to seven. London: OfSTED Publications.

O'Hanlon, C. 2000 The emotionally competent school: a step towards school improvement and raising standards. Management in Education, 14, 2, pp22-24

Ooi YP, Lam CM, Sung M, Tan WT, Goh TJ, Fung DS, Pathy P, Ang RP, Chua A. 2008 Effects of cognitive-behavioural therapy on anxiety for children with high-functioning autistic spectrum disorders. Singapore Med J. 49:215–20

Oxford University Press. 18 October 2012 http://oxforddictionaries.com/definition/english/detention April 2010

Pavlov, I. P. 1897/1902. The Work Of The Digestive Glands. London: Griffin

Paxton, K. and Estay, I.A. 2007. Counselling People on the Autism Spectrum: A Practical Manual. London: Jessica Kingsley.

Perry, D.W., Marston, G.M., Hinder, S.A.J., Munden, A.C. and Roy, A. 2001. The phenomenology of depressive illness in people with a learning disability and autism.
Autism, 5, (3), 265-275

Qualifications and Curriculum Authority, 2005. The P Scales – Level descriptors P1 to P8 London: Qualifications and Curriculum Authority

Ramin, E. (2011). The Implementation of Life Space Crisis Intervention as a School-Wide Strategy for Reducing Violence and Supporting Students' Continuation in Public Schools. Teaching and Leadership: Dissertations. Paper 235.

Redl, F. (1960). Strategy and Techniques of the Life Space Interview. American Journal of Orthopsychiatry.

Royal College of Psychiatrists, 2012. RCPsych Public Education Editorial Board
http://www.rcpsych.ac.uk/mentalhealthinfo/treatments/cbt.aspx 04.07.12

Scope, 2012. http://www.scope.org.uk/help-and-information/communication 20.6.12

Scope, 2012. http://www.scope.org.uk/help-and-information/publications/communication-passport 20.6.12

Sellman, Edward (2009) 'Lessons learned: student voice at a school for pupils experiencing social, emotional and behavioural difficulties', Emotional and Behavioural Difficulties,14:1,33 — 48

Siegal, D. & Bryson, T.P. (2014). No-Drama Discipline: The Whole-Brain Way to Calm the Chaos and Nurture Your Child's Developing Mind. (New York: Bantam).

Skinner, B. F. (1990). The non-punitive society. Japanese Journal of Behavior Analysis, 5, 98-106.

Smallwood, Beverly. (2010). The Terrible Effects of Deliberate Humiliation. Available: http://www.hodu.com/humiliation.shtml. Last accessed 26 Jul 2010.

Smith, BA (2005). Saturday detention as an effective disciplinary consequence: High school administrators' perspective" (January 1, 2005). Dissertations Collection for University of Connecticut. Paper AAI3180258.

Sofronoff, K., Attwood, T. and Hinton, S. 2005. A randomised controlled trial of a CBT intervention for anxiety in children with Asperger syndrome. Journal of Child Psychology and Psychiatry, 46: 1152–1160. doi: 10.1111/j.1469-7610.2005.00411.x

Syed, M (2015) Black Box Thinking. London: John Murray

Taylor, A.S. 2000. The UN Convention on the Rights of the Child: Giving children a voice. Researching children's perspectives, ed. A. Lewis and G. Lindsay. Buckingham: Open University Press

Thomas, G. (2009) How to do your Research Project. London: SAGE Publications Ltd

Thorley G (2000) Behavioural difficulties in Law J (eds) Communication difficulties in childhood Oxford: Radcliffe Medical Press:

Tversky, A. and Kahneman, D., 1989. Rational choice and the framing of decisions (pp. 81-126). Springer Berlin Heidelberg.

Van Bockern, S. Ashworth, J. Ailts, J. Donnelly, J. Erickson, K. and Woltermann, J. (2008). The restorative justice centre: an alternative to school detention. Reclaiming Children and Youth. 17(3):22-27.

Van Bockern, S. Ashworth, J. Ailts, J. Donnelly, J. Erickson, K. Tobin, T. and Sugai, G.(1996). Patterns in middle school discipline records. Journal of Emotional and Behavioural Disorders, 4, 82–95.

Vermeulen, P. and Vanspranghe, E. 2006. Psychological Support of Individuals with an Autistic Spectrum Disorder. Good Autism Practice, 7, 1, 23-29

Weare, K. and Gray, G. 2003. What works in developing children's emotional and social competence and well-being? Nottingham: Department for Education and Skills.

White-McMahon, W. (2009) The Effects of Life Space Crisis Intervention on Troubled Students' Socio-emotional Growth and Development. Manitoba: Walden University

Wood, M. and Long, NJ.(1991) Life space intervention. Talking with children in crisis. Austin: Pro-Ed.

Wood, T and Berry, B (2003) Editorial, What does "Design Research" Offer Mathematics Teacher Education?, Journal of Mathematics Teacher Education 6 pp195-199

Wood, J. J., Drahota, A., Sze, K., Har, K., Chiu, A. and Langer, D. A. 2009. Cognitive behavioural therapy for anxiety in children with autism spectrum disorders: a randomized, controlled trial. Journal of Child Psychology and Psychiatry, 50: 224–234. doi: 10.1111/j.1469-7610.2008.01948.x

Made in the USA
Columbia, SC
09 June 2017